W9-BOC-933

130574

WORLD HISTORY SERIES ■ ■ ■

Ancient
Greece

by
Don Nardo

Lucent Books, P.O. Box 289011, San Diego, CA 92198-9011

Titles in The World History Series

The Age of Feudalism	The Hundred Years War
Ancient Greece	The Roman Empire
The French and Indian War	The Roman Republic
Hitler's Reich	The Russian Revolution

Library of Congress Cataloging-in-Publication Data

Nardo, Don, 1947–
    Ancient Greece / by Don Nardo.
        p.   cm.—(World history series)
    Includes bibliographical references and index.
    Summary: Traces the history of Greek civilization from the
rise of the city-states to the flourishing of the classical Greek
empire.
    ISBN 1-56006-229-0
    1. Greece—Civilization—To 146 B.C.—Juvenile literature.
[1. Greece—History—to 146 B.C. 2. Greece—Civilization—To
146 B.C.]   I. Title.   II. Series.
DF77.N37   1994
938—dc20   93-6904
                                                                                    CIP
                                                                                    AC

Copyright 1994 by Lucent Books, Inc., P.O. Box 289011, San
Diego, California, 92198-9011

No part of this book may be reproduced or used in any other
form or by any other means, electrical, mechanical, or otherwise, including, but not limited to photocopy, recording, or any
information storage and retrieval system, without prior written
permission from the publisher.

Printed in the USA

Contents

Foreword   4
Important Dates in Ancient Greece   6

INTRODUCTION
A Simple and Noble Concept   9

CHAPTER 1
The Age of Heroes: The Birth of Greek Civilization   11

CHAPTER 2
The Rise of City-States: Prelude to the Classic Age   22

CHAPTER 3
West Versus East: The Greek and Persian Wars   34

CHAPTER 4
Athenian Empire: Power and Expansion
Inflame Old Rivalries   44

CHAPTER 5
Cultural Outburst: The Golden Age of Athens   55

CHAPTER 6
Greek Versus Greek: The Peloponnesian War   66

CHAPTER 7
Alexander's Conquests: The Spread of Greek Culture   76

CHAPTER 8
The Hellenistic Age: The Decline of the Greeks   87

EPILOGUE
The Greek Spirit Lives On   95

Notes   99
For Further Reading   102
Works Consulted   103
Index   106
Picture Credits   111
About the Author   112

Foreword

Each year on the first day of school, nearly every history teacher faces the task of explaining why his or her students should study history. One logical answer to this question is that exploring what happened in our past explains how the things we often take for granted—our customs, ideas, and institutions—came to be. As statesman and historian Winston Churchill put it, "Every nation or group of nations has its own tale to tell. Knowledge of the trials and struggles is necessary to all who would comprehend the problems, perils, challenges, and opportunities which confront us today." Thus, a study of history puts modern ideas and institutions in perspective. For example, though the founders of the United States were talented and creative thinkers, they clearly did not invent the concept of democracy. Instead, they adapted some democratic ideas that had originated in ancient Greece and with which the Romans, the British, and others had experimented. An exploration of these cultures, then, reveals their very real connection to us through institutions that continue to shape our daily lives.

Another reason often given for studying history is the idea that lessons exist in the past from which contemporary societies can benefit and learn. This idea, although controversial, has always been an intriguing one for historians. Those that agree that society can benefit from the past often quote philosopher George Santayana's famous statement, "Those who cannot remember the past are condemned to repeat it." Historians who ascribe to Santayana's philosophy believe that, for example, studying the events that led up to the major world wars or other significant historical events would allow society to chart a different and more favorable course in the future.

Just as difficult as convincing students to realize the importance of studying history is the search for useful and interesting supplementary materials that present historical events in a context that can be easily understood. The volumes in Lucent Books' World History Series attempt to present a broad, balanced, and penetrating view of the march of history. Ancient Egypt's important wars and rulers, for example, are presented against the rich and colorful backdrop of Egyptian religious, social, and cultural developments. The series engages the reader by enhancing historical events with these cultural contexts. For example, in *Ancient Greece,* the text covers the role of women in that society. Slavery is discussed in *The Roman Empire,* as well as how slaves earned their freedom. The numerous and varied aspects of everyday life in these and other societies are explored in each volume of the series. Additionally, the series covers the major political, cultural, and philosophical ideas as the torch of civilization is passed from ancient Mesopotamia and Egypt, through Greece, Rome, Medieval Europe, and other world cultures, to the modern day.

The material in the series is formatted in a thorough, precise, and organized manner. Each volume offers the reader a comprehensive and clearly written overview of an important historical event or period. The topic under discussion is placed in a broad, historical context. For example, *The Italian Renaissance* begins with a discussion of the High Middle Ages and the loss of central control that allowed certain Italian cities to develop artistically. The book ends by looking forward to the Reformation and interpreting the societal changes that grew out of the Renaissance. Thus, students are not only involved in an historical era, but also enveloped by the events leading up to that era and the events following it.

One important and unique feature in the World History Series is the primary and secondary source quotations that richly supplement each volume. These quotes are useful in a number of ways. First, they allow students access to sources they would not normally be exposed to because of the difficulty and obscurity of the original source. The quotations range from interesting anecdotes to far-sighted cultural perspectives and are drawn from historical witnesses both past and present. Second, the quotes demonstrate how and where historians themselves derive their information on the past as they strive to reach a consensus on historical events. Lastly, all of the quotes are footnoted, familiarizing students with the citation process and allowing them to verify quotes and/or look up the original source if the quote piques their interest.

Finally, the books in the World History Series provide a detailed launching point for further research. Each book contains a bibliography specifically geared toward student research. A second, annotated bibliography introduces students to all the sources the author consulted when compiling the book. A chronology of important dates gives students an overview, at a glance, of the topic covered. Where applicable, a glossary of terms is included.

In short, the series is designed not only to acquaint readers with the basics of history, but also to make them aware that their lives are a part of an ongoing human saga. Perhaps they will then come to the same realization as famed historian Arnold Toynbee. In his monumental work, *A Study of History*, he wrote about becoming aware of history flowing through him in a mighty current, and of his own life "welling like a wave in the flow of this vast tide."

Important Dates in Ancient Greece

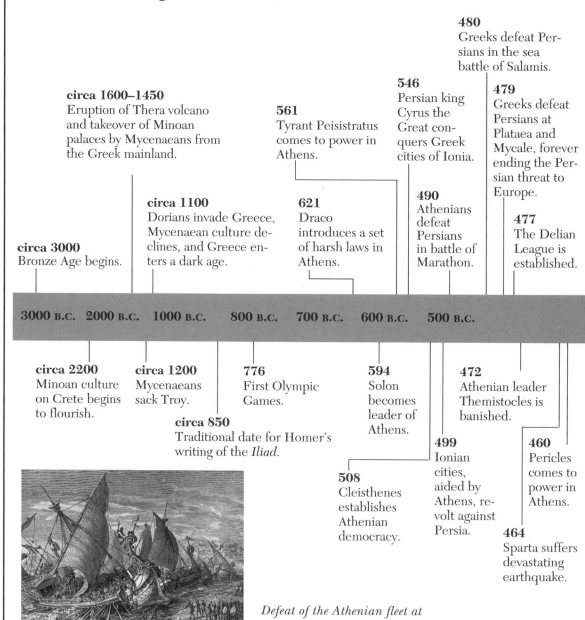

circa 1600–1450
Eruption of Thera volcano and takeover of Minoan palaces by Mycenaeans from the Greek mainland.

480
Greeks defeat Persians in the sea battle of Salamis.

546
Persian king Cyrus the Great conquers Greek cities of Ionia.

479
Greeks defeat Persians at Plataea and Mycale, forever ending the Persian threat to Europe.

561
Tyrant Peisistratus comes to power in Athens.

circa 1100
Dorians invade Greece, Mycenaean culture declines, and Greece enters a dark age.

621
Draco introduces a set of harsh laws in Athens.

490
Athenians defeat Persians in battle of Marathon.

477
The Delian League is established.

circa 3000
Bronze Age begins.

3000 B.C. **2000 B.C.** **1000 B.C.** **800 B.C.** **700 B.C.** **600 B.C.** **500 B.C.**

circa 2200
Minoan culture on Crete begins to flourish.

circa 1200
Mycenaeans sack Troy.

776
First Olympic Games.

594
Solon becomes leader of Athens.

472
Athenian leader Themistocles is banished.

circa 850
Traditional date for Homer's writing of the *Iliad*.

499
Ionian cities, aided by Athens, revolt against Persia.

460
Pericles comes to power in Athens.

508
Cleisthenes establishes Athenian democracy.

464
Sparta suffers devastating earthquake.

Defeat of the Athenian fleet at Syracuse in 413 B.C.

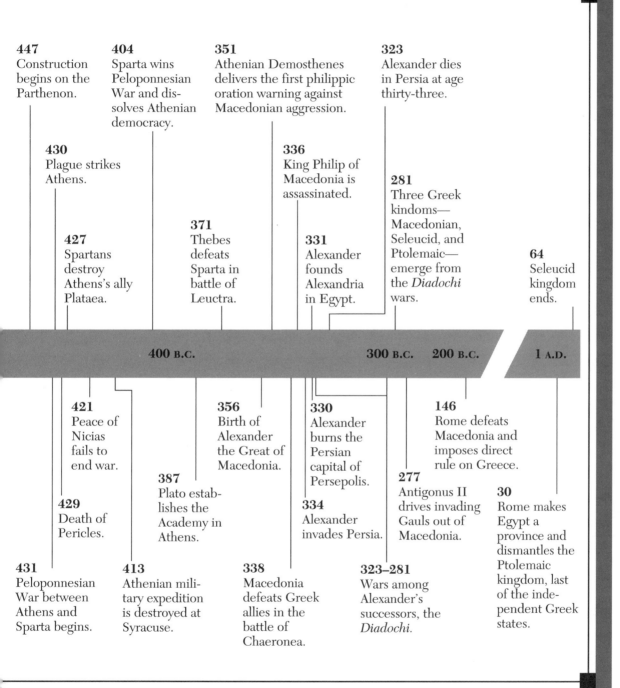

447
Construction begins on the Parthenon.

430
Plague strikes Athens.

427
Spartans destroy Athens's ally Plataea.

404
Sparta wins Peloponnesian War and dissolves Athenian democracy.

371
Thebes defeats Sparta in battle of Leuctra.

351
Athenian Demosthenes delivers the first philippic oration warning against Macedonian aggression.

336
King Philip of Macedonia is assassinated.

331
Alexander founds Alexandria in Egypt.

323
Alexander dies in Persia at age thirty-three.

281
Three Greek kindoms—Macedonian, Seleucid, and Ptolemaic—emerge from the *Diadochi* wars.

64
Seleucid kingdom ends.

400 B.C.   300 B.C.   200 B.C.   1 A.D.

421
Peace of Nicias fails to end war.

429
Death of Pericles.

431
Peloponnesian War between Athens and Sparta begins.

413
Athenian military expedition is destroyed at Syracuse.

387
Plato establishes the Academy in Athens.

356
Birth of Alexander the Great of Macedonia.

338
Macedonia defeats Greek allies in the battle of Chaeronea.

334
Alexander invades Persia.

330
Alexander burns the Persian capital of Persepolis.

323–281
Wars among Alexander's successors, the *Diadochi*.

277
Antigonus II drives invading Gauls out of Macedonia.

146
Rome defeats Macedonia and imposes direct rule on Greece.

30
Rome makes Egypt a province and dismantles the Ptolemaic kingdom, last of the independent Greek states.

A Simple and Noble Concept

When examining the colorful, exciting panorama of ancient Greek civilization, it is easy to become swept up in the drama of events. The tales of the heroes of the Trojan War battling with bronze swords and spears before the towering stone walls of Troy still capture people's imagination. The brilliant rise and tragic fall of ancient Athens, a great city with magnificent temples, sculptures, and theaters, remains a fascinating and moving story. And the brave stand made by King Leonidas and his 300 Spartans against an army of more than 200,000 Persians continues to thrill and excite people.

But such events and achievements are only part of Greece's history. The Greeks left behind for later cultures more than a gripping saga of events and the decaying remnants of great art and architecture.

Athens as it looked during the reign of Roman emperor Hadrian when Greece was part of the Roman Empire.

In this painting by the nineteenth century French painter Jean Gerome, Greek actors lounge backstage before a performance.

Greek ideas—for example, the belief that the truths of nature are not beyond the grasp of the human mind but are learnable—have survived through the centuries. These ideas became some of the fundamental concepts of modern science, government, and philosophy. Many people today take for granted these concepts without realizing that they originated with the Greeks.

The simplest yet perhaps most significant idea developed and passed on by the Greeks is the belief that the individual is both important and special. As historian C. M. Bowra explained, "At the center of the Greek outlook lay an unshakable belief in the worth of the individual man. In centuries when large parts of the earth were dominated by . . . absolute monarchies . . . the Greeks were evolving their belief that a man must be respected not as the instrument of an omnipotent overlord, but for his own sake."[1]

In ancient lands like Egypt and Mesopotamia, a few kings held absolute power over all of the people. From birth to death, the common person lived only to serve the needs and desires of the ruler. Since the concept of individual rights did not exist in these lands, common people had no say in their government, no outlet for individual expression, and no feeling of self-worth.

In Greece, by contrast, the recognition of the worth of the individual opened up whole new avenues of thought and action. People came to believe that their own needs and desires were important and that they had a right to shape their own destiny. From this view evolved the concept of democracy, the rule by and for the people. Individual creative expression also blossomed, leading to great achievements in art, literature, and philosophy. In addition, the Greeks paved the way for the development of science with their belief that the power of an individual's mind could reveal the truths of nature. It is important to note that some Greeks—women, for example—were not allowed individual expression or the right to take part in government. But the fact that a sizable segment of the population did enjoy these rights was bold and revolutionary at the time.

The great and complex drama of Greek history, which still inspires and enriches the modern world, was driven largely by the simple and noble concept of human individuality. "Through their respect for the individual and the power of the individual's mind," commented historian Charles Alexander Robinson, the Greeks "created one of the greatest civilizations in the history of the world."[2]

Chapter

1 The Age of Heroes: The Birth of Greek Civilization

Jutting down from southern Europe into the eastern Mediterranean Sea is the arid, mountainous land of Greece. Though small—only about the size of New York State—Greece has greatly contributed to the development of human culture. In the sixth, fifth, and fourth centuries B.C., the Greeks created a brilliant and remarkable civilization. Referred to today as the Classic Age, this was the era when Greek art, architecture, and philosophy reached their peak. It was the Greece of Pericles, the distinguished statesman and builder, of great playwrights such as Aeschylus and Sophocles, and of original thinkers like Socrates and Plato. The influence of this magnificent culture on later cultures was profound and long-lasting. Greek art and ideas helped

In this fanciful depiction of an unidentified Greek city, the citizens cheer the return of a victorious fleet.

shape Western, or European-based, civilization, and they remain a powerful inspiration to people around the world today.

The appearance of the splendid culture of classical Greece was not a sudden or chance occurrence. Instead, it grew out of many centuries of Greek civilization stretching back into the Bronze Age—the era in southern Europe from about 3000 to 1000 B.C. in which people used weapons and tools made of bronze. The classical Greeks called this dimly remembered period in their past the Age of Heroes.

At the Dawn of the Western World

The first advanced culture in Greece, and indeed in all of Europe, was created by a people referred to today as the Minoans. Their civilization flourished from about 2200 to 1450 B.C. on Crete, the large island located about one hundred miles southeast of the Greek mainland. The Minoans built huge, splendid palaces. For example, the palace at Knossos, their chief city, located near the northern coast of the island, was five stories high and consisted of hundreds of interconnected rooms. The Minoans erected palaces similar to the one at Knossos at other Cretan sites, such as Phaestos and Mallia. There is evidence that these were highly sophisticated buildings with modern-style plumbing features, such as flush toilets and clay pipes carrying hot and cold water. As many as thirty to fifty thousand people lived in the palace at Knossos and in the city that surrounded it. And there were dozens, perhaps hundreds, of Minoan cities and towns on Crete and the islands of the Aegean Sea, the inlet of the Mediterranean Sea bordering eastern Greece.

With a vast fleet of ships, these cities carried on a prosperous trade with one another and also with nearby foreign lands like Egypt. In addition to being expert sailors, the Minoans were brilliant artists. They decorated their palaces and houses with many exquisite frescoes, which are paintings and murals done on wet plaster.

Part of a street excavated at Akrotiri, an ash-buried Minoan town discovered on Thera in the 1960s by Greek archaeologist Spyridon Marinatos.

What little is known about Minoan religion indicates that these early Greeks, unlike most other ancient peoples, envisioned their gods as gentle and nurturing, rather than overpowering and vengeful. "There were no vast portraits of the gods," remarked historian Robert Payne. "Indeed, there were scarcely any gods, and the few that were discovered usually took the form of pottery figurines only a few inches high. . . . They painted no goblins, no demons, no dark gods."[3] Of the few humanlike deities the Minoans worshiped, most were female. Among the most important were the Great Mother, who ruled over the heavens and the earth, and the Mistress of the Animals, often depicted by artists as standing on a mountaintop.

The Minoans also worshiped bulls. Paintings and carvings show Minoan youths vaulting over the backs of sacred bulls in a combination of sport and religious ritual. Male and female vaulters competed on equal terms. The bull vaulters and the spectators who watched them appear to have greatly enjoyed the thrill of danger these games provided.

The same gender equality was seen in the Minoans' social life. Men and women often exchanged their opinions in markets or other public places. This and other evidence suggests that Minoan women enjoyed near or total equality with men. This was unheard-of anywhere else in the ancient world, even in the enlightened society of the classical Greeks, in which women had to do the bidding of men.

The Minoans appear to have been peaceful and happy. Surviving Minoan frescoes and jewelry carvings frequently show people relaxing, fishing, and playing games. The scenes depict a prosperous, creative people with abundant curiosity and a zest for life. The Minoans, said Robert Payne,

demonstrated that they were no longer bound helplessly to the fearful gods. They walked with their eyes wide open, and they were unafraid. Those frescoes and jewels dug out of the earth speak to us directly across the centuries, and we recognize our kinship to these people who stand at the dawn of the Western world. They had an innocence which we have lost, and a delighted awareness of the springs of life which is almost beyond our comprehension.[4]

Unearthing the Truth Behind the Legend

Because the Minoans kept few records and no histories, their culture had been largely forgotten by the time of the classical Greeks. Yet a few vague memories of Minoan days remained, passed on by word of mouth over the course of many centuries. Exaggerated and romanticized by repeated tellings, some Minoan cities, people, and events survived as legends and myths. After the decline of classical Greece, most people assumed that these myths were purely fanciful. Only in modern times did archaeologists, scientists who dig up artifacts and study past civilizations, discover that many of these stories had a basis in fact.

Perhaps the most famous myth about Minoan times concerned King Minos, who ruled a great kingdom from his splendid palace in the city of Knossos. Even cities on the Greek mainland, such as Athens, came under his domination. Under Minos's palace, in a huge maze called the Labyrinth, dwelled his son, the Minotaur, a monster

The Athenian hero Theseus rescues Ariadne and the Athenian captives.
Note the bull-symbol of the monstrous Minotaur on the wall.

that was half-human and half-bull. The king regularly appeased the fearsome creature by feeding it young Athenian men and women. Eventually, an Athenian hero named Theseus traveled to Crete, determined to kill the Minotaur. As the ancient Greek historian Plutarch described it:

> When he arrived in Crete . . . having a clue of thread given him by Ariadne [Minos's daughter], who had fallen in love with him, and being instructed by her how to use it so as to conduct him through the wanderings of the labyrinth [by unraveling it as he walked], he escaped out of it and slew the Minotaur, and sailed back, taking along with him Ariadne and the young Athenian captives.[5]

For dozens of centuries, the tale of Minos's palace and monstrous offspring remained mere myth. Then, in the year 1900, the British archaeologist Sir Arthur Evans began excavating at the legendary site of Knossos. He discovered the remains of a palace and reasoned that it could easily have served as a model for the mythical labyrinth. The palace was adorned with numerous paintings and sculptures depicting bull worship. Evans and other scholars suggested that priests wearing bull's horns or masks may have inspired the myth of the half-human Minotaur. Because the evidence found at Knossos conformed to the legend of King Minos so closely, Evans dubbed the early Greeks who built the city Minoan.

Mainland Builders and Raiders

During the same centuries that the Minoans thrived on Crete, another group of early Greeks, the Mycenaeans, lived on the Greek mainland. Their name comes from their chief fortress-city of Mycenae, located in a hilly area of southeastern Greece. Other Mycenaean towns, including Tiryns, Pilos, and Athens, each ruled by its own king, dotted southern Greece. "The Mycenaeans," said C. M. Bowra, "were spectacular builders. Their palaces were built within formidable citadels with

This tholos, *or beehive tomb, at Mycenae is often referred to as the "Treasury of Atreus."*

walls 10 feet thick, and some of their royal tombs were enormous beehive structures made of stones weighing, sometimes, as much as 120 tons."[6] The stones were so large, in fact, that the classical Greeks who later visited the ruins of Mycenae thought that they had been built by a giant race.

For a long time, the Minoans on Crete influenced and dominated the Mycenaeans on the mainland. Mainland customs, styles of dress, and religion conformed to those of Crete. The two peoples also spoke a common language, an early form of Greek.

The major difference between the Minoans and Mycenaeans was that Mycenaean society was more regimented, militaristic, and warlike than its Cretan counterpart. Although both Minoans and Mycenaeans were traders, the Mycenaeans were also pirates and raiders who attacked neighboring peoples. For a long time, the aggressive Mycenaeans dominated only the mainland. As long as the powerful Minoan navy controlled the Aegean, the Mycenaeans had no hope of expanding southward and eastward.

A Deadly Mountain Springs to Life

The balance of power in Bronze Age Greece shifted drastically sometime between 1600 and 1450 B.C. when a natural disaster of unparalleled destructive force struck the Minoan world. On the tiny round island of Thera about seventy miles north of Crete lay one of the most important Minoan cities. Unknown to the Minoans, however, Thera was the summit of a giant underwater volcano. After thousands of years of inactivity, the mountain suddenly sprang to life and spewed millions of

These vases at Akrotiri rest in the exact positions they were in when the Thera volcano buried them and the entire town sometime between 1600 and 1450 B.C.

tons of ash, darkening the skies over much of the eastern Mediterranean. The volcano then collapsed violently, forming a huge circular depression called a caldera. Aegean scholar J. V. Luce summed up the enormous power of this event, saying that one can

> think in terms of an explosion heard from one end of the Mediterranean to the other. One may suppose that the blast damaged houses on Crete and on the surrounding islands over a radius of at least 150 km. [90 miles], and possibly much further. . . . The eruption is likely to have been accompanied by violent electrical storms and torrential rain. Next one must think of the devastating effect of huge tidal waves associated with the final paroxysmal [disastrous] outburst. . . . It is virtually certain that the convulsions attending the formation of the caldera must have been accompanied by an enormous displacement of water. It is possible to think in terms of vast mountains of water, perhaps 60 to 100 m. [200 to 330 feet] high, moving shoreward at velocities of up to 160 km. [96 miles] per hour. The thickly populated northern coast of Crete, with its many important settlements lying on or near the shore, . . . suffered most severely.[7]

The Thera eruption, the worst natural disaster in recorded history, toppled the Minoan palaces and must have destroyed much of the fleet. It is likely that thousands died from drowning and thousands more of starvation after the rain of volcanic ash ruined much of the region's agriculture. The catastrophe was so terrible that the memory of it became part of the legends passed down through the generations to the classical Greeks. More than one thousand years after the catastrophe, the Greek philosopher Plato recorded these legends in his tale of Atlantis, a great seafaring island nation that sank into the sea in a single day.

The Trojan War

Despite the severity of the disaster, the Minoan culture survived and might have slowly been rebuilt had it not been for the ambitious Mycenaeans. With their neighbors temporarily weakened, the mainlanders invaded Crete and the Aegean islands and took over the Minoan settlements. The Mycenaeans rebuilt some of the ruined palaces and continued to practice Minoan customs and religion.

But while the Minoans had traded peacefully with cities on nearby Mediterranean coasts, the new rulers of the Aegean world

---

Wrath of the Stone God

The eruption of the volcano on the Aegean island of Thera sometime between 1600 and 1450 B.C. was the most destructive natural disaster in recorded history. In this excerpt from Unearthing Atlantis: An Archaeological Odyssey, *marine archaeologist Charles Pellegrino, who has extensively studied the volcano, poetically describes aspects of the catastrophe that helped bring about the end of the splendid Minoan culture:*

"There is a place where a stone god rose up from the sea and a mountain opened up in the sky; and as the world heaved and compressed, there occurred sights and sounds of which today's foremost nuclear weapons designers scarcely dream. I know of a world that saw waves as high as skyscrapers. I know of a cloud that spread globular and huge, and where it touched the earth and the sea, it converted men into gas. I know of a rend in the earth more than seven miles wide. It is flooded with water now, and if you were to stand in a boat near its center, your mind would resist coming to terms with the size of it, would try to reject the idea that such a thing could be carved out in a single day and night. I know of a city near the rend, nearly four thousand years old and buried, in places, under more than two hundred feet of ash. . . . The homes had running water and bathtubs and flush toilets; and it seems possible that the bedrooms were heated in the wintertime by steam piped in from volcanic vents, as it traveled on to rooftop cisterns, where it was condensed for bathwater. If any were caught sleeping in those warm rooms when the volcano awoke, they were fortunate, in a fashion—more fortunate than the hundreds of thousands of their fellow Atlanteans on the shores of Crete. . . . For they, at least, died without understanding that they were the last of the true Minoans, that their entire civilization had just been set upon the wane [decline]."

Archaeologists believe that the original Theran towns looked very similar to this modern one.

now raided and plundered these same cities. For nearly three centuries, the Mycenaeans crossed the Aegean and launched military expeditions against the islands and coasts of Asia Minor, what is now Turkey.

One of these expeditions turned out to be the most important and famous event in Mycenaean history. About 1200 B.C., the Mycenaeans attacked and burned Troy, an independent trading city located on the northwestern coast of Asia Minor. The city must have had considerable political and economic importance at the time because most Mycenaean kings took part in the siege. They were led by Agamemnon, king of Mycenae. The event was significant because it was the only time that so many Mycenaean kingdoms united in a common effort.

The siege of Troy had even greater significance because its story became the basis of classical Greek literature and religion.

The war also became the chief symbol of Greek unity and cultural pride. Later Greeks knew about the Trojan War because memories of the event were preserved in stories and poems passed on through the centuries by word of mouth. Traveling poets, called bards, excited audiences with tales of the great Greek heroes who crossed the "wine dark sea" and fought before the towering walls of "windy Troy."

According to the poems, the Greeks fought to rescue Helen, wife of King Menelaus of Sparta, after she had been abducted by Paris, a Trojan prince. The siege lasted ten years, and the Greeks finally used a trick to gain entrance into the city. They constructed a huge wooden horse, gave it to the Trojans as a gift, then pretended to leave. The Trojans dragged the horse into Troy, unaware that Greek warriors were hiding inside. That night, as the Trojans slept, the Greeks climbed out of the horse and opened the gates for their army.

A woodcut depicts the Trojan horse from thirteenth century Sicilian poet Guido delle Colonne's Trojan History.

Epic Adventure Tales

As the bards told, retold, and embellished the stories of the Trojan War, the exploits of warriors like Achilles, Ajax, and Odysseus became long, complex, and fanciful sagas. In these epics, the Greek gods often interacted with mortals and even took sides in the war. The most important surviving epic poems are the *Iliad* and the *Odyssey*. The *Iliad* tells the story of the Trojan War, while the *Odyssey* recounts the fantastic adventures of the warrior Odysseus on his way home from the war. Both are attributed to a legendary bard named Homer, who may have lived about 850 B.C. But it is clear that Homer did not invent these stories. Possibly, he was the most talented and popular of the bards to tell them.

A European engraving of Homer, author of the Iliad, *based solely on the artist's imagination.*

When eventually written down, these exciting adventure tales represented the first important examples of European literature. Because they described the gods and their exploits in such detail, Homer's tales also became the original sourcebooks for the religion of the classical Greeks. Nearly every Greek child could recite by heart passages from the *Iliad* such as the one in which the goddess Athena spurred the Greek soldiers into battle:

> King Agamemnon . . . gave immediate orders to his clear-voiced heralds to call the long-haired Achaeans [Greeks] to battle. . . . With them went Athena of the Flashing Eyes, wearing her splendid cloak . . . from which a hundred golden tassels flutter. . . . Resplendent [magnificent-looking] in this, she flew through the ranks, urging the men forward; and in each one she inspired the will to carry on the war and fight relentlessly.[8]

Until modern times, scholars thought the city of Troy and Homer's epic about its fall were totally fictional. Then, in 1870, the German archaeologist Heinrich Schliemann excavated a mound on the coast of Turkey and discovered the remains of the legendary fortress-city. Schliemann proved that the fabulous story of the Trojan War was, to some degree, based on real cities, people, and events.

A History Half-Forgotten

Evidence found by Schliemann and other scholars shows that the attack on Troy was one of the last successful ventures of the

Achilles Slays Hector

Homer's monumental epic poem the Iliad *describes the events and characters of the last six weeks of the ten-year Greek siege of Troy, a real event that occurred about 1200 B.C. It is a long, complex, and colorful tale filled with battles, intrigue, and the exploits of many heroes. Yet the story centers primarily on the character of the Greek warrior Achilles, a brave, almost invincible, yet moody and impulsive man whose pride and anger bring about his own downfall. In the following excerpt, from a translation by W. H. D. Rouse, Achilles fights Hector, one of the princes of Troy. Hector had earlier slain Patroclos, Achilles' friend, and now Achilles seeks his revenge, saying:*

"'Hector, I cannot forget. . . . Call up your manhood; now you surely need to be a spearman and a bold man of war. There is no chance of escape now. . . . Now in one lump sum you shall pay for all my companions, whom you have slain and I have mourned.' With the words he poised and cast his long spear. But Hector saw it coming and crouched down, so that it flew over and struck in the earth.

'A miss! [shouted Hector]. . . . You are only a rattle-tongue . . . trying to frighten me and make me lose heart. . . . I will charge you straight, and then you may strike me in the breast if it be God's will, but first see if you can avoid *my* spear.' . . . He poised his spear and cast it, and hit the shield fair in the middle; but the spear rebounded and fell away. . . . He drew the sword that hung by his side . . . gathered himself and sprang. . . . Achilles moved to meet him full of fury, covering his chest with the resplendent [magnificent] shield while the thick golden plumes nodded upon his flashing helmet. . . . He scanned Hector with a ruthless heart, to see where the white flesh gave the best opening for a blow. Hector was well covered with that splendid armour which he had stript from Patroclos, but an opening showed . . . the gullet. . . . There Achilles aimed, and the point went through the soft neck. . . .

Hector . . . fell in the dust, and Achilles cried in triumph: 'There, Hector! . . . Now you shall be mauled by vultures and dogs. . . . For what you have done to me I wish from the bottom of my heart that I could cut you to pieces and eat you raw myself!' He drew the spear from the body and laid it aside. Then he stript off the armour. . . . And then he thought of a shameful outrage. He cut behind the sinews of both Hector's feet from ankle to heel and strapt them together with leather thongs, and fastened them to his chariot leaving the head to drag. Then he laid the armour in the car, and got in himself and whipt up the horses. Away they flew: the dust rose as the body was dragged along."

This depiction of Heinrich Schliemann's nineteenth century excavation of Troy appeared in Schliemann's book Troy and Its Remains.

Mycenaeans. About 1100 B.C., a more primitive Greek-speaking people called the Dorians swept down from what is now northern Greece. The Dorians had iron weapons, which were stronger and more effective than the Mycenaeans' bronze swords and spears. The invaders destroyed the Mycenaean cities and, instead of rebuilding them, lived as squatters in the ruins. Most surviving Mycenaeans fled southward and westward and settled on the islands and coasts of Asia Minor, a region the Greeks later called Ionia. The only mainland city that survived the savage Dorian onslaught was Athens, located on a peninsula called Attica on the east coast. There, a few Mycenaeans continued to carry on their old ways. But in time, these ways changed and disappeared. Mycenaean writing, record keeping, and most arts and handicrafts vanished, even in Athens and Ionia.

Greece entered a dark age, a period of about three hundred years about which

scholars know very little. During these centuries, the memories of many of the events and heroes of the Bronze Age lived on. But, as historian Stringfellow Barr said, "It was a history that had been half forgotten and that had been transmuted into poetry, so that the history of many centuries of Minoan culture, of Mycenaean power, of . . . Dorian invaders from the north, of . . . the great crusade to Troy . . . this history became scrambled, jumbled."[9] And so, the magnificent Minoan-Mycenaean world passed into legend. Over the generations, the surviving Greeks, Dorian and Mycenaean alike, forgot their heritage and identified themselves only with the particular valley or island where they lived. They became poor farmers, fishermen, and shepherds. But the glory of Aegean culture was not over. In time, the Greeks would build a new civilization, one that would greatly surpass that of the heroes that inspired them.

2 The Rise of City-States: Prelude to the Classic Age

During the three centuries that followed the Dorian invasion in 1100 B.C., Greek civilization reached its lowest point. When the Minoan and Mycenaean cultures disappeared, so too did their prosperous trade network, writing, arts, architecture, and most crafts. The Dorians, who possessed few such civilized skills, were contented to carry on their primitive tribal culture.

Along with cultural stagnation came widespread poverty. Before, foreign commerce and raiding expeditions had regularly brought grains and other foodstuffs into Greece, supplementing local agricul-

ture. But now, people had to subsist solely on whatever crops they could grow or animals they could raise. Because Greece is a dry, rocky, infertile land, few crops grow well in its soil. The people had to work nearly from sunup to sundown just to eke out a meager living. Only very slowly, over the course of centuries, did commerce revive, first among the Greeks themselves and later with other peoples. It was not until the eighth century B.C. that living standards began to reach levels comparable to those before the Dorian assault.

The rear of the Athenian Acropolis, showing the rocky cliff on which it was built.

One Land with Many Nations

Greece's terrain, riddled with many mountains, valleys, and islands, profoundly affected the development of Greek culture during and after the dark age. Everywhere, small groups of people clung to their local valleys and islands. In these sheltered environments, many different societies evolved, each consisting of a central town surrounded by small villages and farmland. Most towns were built around a hill or cliff called an acropolis, which means "high place of the city" in Greek. People fortified their acropolis to defend

Evolution of the Acropolis and Marketplace

The acropolis, translated as "high place of the town," and the central marketplace were the two most important features of Greek cities. In this excerpt from The Greeks, *historian and scholar H. D. F. Kitto explains how these developed during the Greek dark age, when individual city-states were evolving:*

"In a period so unsettled the inhabitants of any valley or island might at a moment's notice be compelled to fight for their fields. Therefore, a local strong-point was necessary, normally a defensible hill-top somewhere in the plain. This, the 'acropolis,' would be fortified, and here would be the residence of the king. It would also be the natural place of assembly, and the religious center. This is the beginning of the town. . . . Natural economic growth made a central market necessary. We saw that the economic system implied by Hesiod and Homer [Greeks who described their own culture] was 'close household economy'; the estate, large or small, produced nearly everything that it needed, and what it could not produce it did without. As things became more stable [however] a rather more specialized economy became possible: more goods were produced for sale. Hence the growth of a market. At this point we may invoke [recall] the very sociable habits of the Greeks, ancient or modern. The English farmer likes to build his house on his land, and to come into town when he has to. What little leisure he has he likes to spend on the very satisfying occupation of looking over a gate. The Greek prefers to live in the town or village, to walk out to his work, and to spend his rather ampler leisure talking in the town or village square. Therefore, the market becomes a market-town, naturally beneath the Acropolis. This became the center of the communal life of the people."

The marketplace in Sparta as it may have looked in the early fourth century B.C.

against attackers in times of war. Although most of these towns were physically similar, their inhabitants developed different customs, governments, and traditions, and they came to think of themselves as separate nations.

This new kind of political unit in Greece was the city-state, a nation built around a single city. By modern standards, these nations were tiny. Even at the height of their development, the largest had a population of only about 200,000, and most had much fewer than 20,000 inhabitants. The Greeks called the city-state the polis (the plural is poleis).

Because the various Greek poleis evolved their own special identities, the concept of individualism became very strong in Greece. In time, the Greeks recognized that just as each city had unique qualities making it worthy of respect, so too did each person. Eventually, after Greece emerged from its dark age, laws were developed to protect the individual, and from these laws the idea of democracy grew.

Linked by Common Origins

Though the hundreds of poleis ruled themselves as separate nations, they also recognized that they shared a common origin and culture. First, they all spoke Greek. Though separate dialects developed in various parts of the land, all Greeks could easily communicate and share ideas. They all called the region they inhabited Hellas and thought of themselves as Hellenes. These names paid homage to Helen of Troy, whose abduction sparked the war that all Greeks recog-

This elaborate representation of Helen of Troy was found at Thessalonica in northern Greece.

nized as the most important event in their history. Their common language, the Greeks felt, separated them from foreigners, whom they referred to as barbarians. At the time, the term *barbarian* was not insulting but merely signified a person who could not speak Greek.

Toward the end of the dark age, sometime around 800 B.C., the Greeks began to

This sculpture of the god Zeus, now in Athens's National Museum, once held a thunderbolt.

Age of Heroes. The story of the *Iliad*, in particular, portrayed the Greeks as banding together into a single army with a common goal. Though the Greeks in the dark age lived separately and often fought with one another, they retained this memory of a time when they were united.

Religion was the most significant cultural link among the Greek states. Worship of the gods was also the single most important aspect of everyday life. During the dark age, tales of various gods from the heroic period survived in myths and epic poems, and people all over Greece came to accept these gods. They recognized Zeus as the chief god. He ruled over both heaven and earth, and his symbols were the thunderbolt and the eagle. Other important gods and goddesses included Apollo, the sun god, who controlled light, truth, music, and poetry; Poseidon, who ruled the seas and caused earthquakes; Aphrodite, goddess of love and beauty; and Artemis, who ruled the night and governed the animals. Most Greeks believed that these gods dwelled on top of Mount Olympus, the highest mountain in Greece, located in the northern region of Thessaly.

use writing again. This time they adopted a set of letters borrowed from a Middle Eastern people called the Phoenicians. Most older languages, including that of the Minoans, used pictures and symbols called pictographs to represent specific words and things. To communicate required learning hundreds or even thousands of separate symbols. The ingenious Phoenicians, however, used a system similar to our own. They used twenty letters, each representing a particular sound. Stringing the letters together in various combinations produced most of the words in a language. The one drawback was that all of the letters were consonants. The combination *mt,* for example, might stand for "mat," "moat," "mitt," or "meet," and the reader had to deduce the meaning from the context of the sentence. The Greeks eliminated this problem by adding vowels to the alphabet.

Another thing all Greeks had in common was their heritage of myths about the

Artemis, goddess of the moon, rides her chariot through the sky.

The Greeks did not envision their gods as perfect deities. The gods, like people, sometimes made mistakes. Also like humans, the Greek gods fought among themselves; had marriages, love affairs, and children; and expressed emotions like hate, pity, and greed. The humanness of the gods did not bother the Greeks. In fact, the Greeks felt that they could relate better to the gods precisely because they acted so much like people. Also, the often frivolous behavior of the gods was much less important to the Greeks than the power these deities had. C. M. Bowra said:

Though Greek gods might seem to modern minds often to fall below the standards demanded of divinity, they had something impressive in common. They were all to a high degree embodiments of power, whether in the physical world or in the mind of man. From them came literally everything, both visible and invisible, and it was the task of the mortals to make the proper use of what the gods provided. The Greeks . . . felt the gods' presence everywhere, especially in times of need such as battle, but equally on high occasions of festival and rejoicing. They thought the gods far more beautiful than men could ever hope to be, and they did not expect them to follow the rules of human behavior. What counted was their power.[10]

Greek Worship

During the centuries in which the Greek city-states evolved and people began to recognize the Olympian gods, ways of wor-shiping these gods also developed. Greek worship was different from that of most other religions, including those practiced today. While most religions are built around a specific moral creed or written set of rules, the Greek religion focused mainly on rituals and ceremonies designed to win the favor of the gods. In Greece, according to historian Will Durant,

there was no church . . . no rigid creed; religion consisted not in professing certain beliefs, but in joining in the official ritual; any man might have his own creed provided that he did not openly deny or blaspheme [insult] the city's gods. . . . The place of worship could be a domestic hearth, the municipal hearth in the city hall . . . some temple for an Olympian god. The ceremony consisted of procession [marching], chants, sacrifice, prayer, and sometimes a sacred meal. . . . Music was essential to the whole process. . . . Having reached the altar—usually in front of the temple—the worshipers sought with sacrifice and prayer to avert the wrath or win the aid of their god.[11]

Each Greek temple was a sacred building dedicated to a specific god who, worshipers believed, visited the building regularly. Even the smallest cities had several temples, and every god had temples scattered throughout Greece.

Eventually, special religious shrines appeared in Greece that all of the various poleis considered their common property. The most important and famous of these was at Delphi, located a few miles north of the Gulf of Corinth in central Greece. The temple at Delphi was dedicated to the god Apollo. People from all over Greece journeyed there to consult the oracle, the shrine's priestess. Most people believed she was a medium through which Apollo and other gods spoke directly to humans. No one knows how the oracles were chosen, but they were always peasant women with no special qualifications. Those seeking advice paid for the oracles' upkeep. A few other Greek shrines had oracles, but none were as revered as those at Delphi.

In time, as commerce began to revive and the poleis became more prosperous, the shrine at Delphi accumulated a vast storehouse of riches. In addition to paying fees, many worshipers brought along fine gifts for Apollo, including precious metals like gold. Also, because the shrine was a sacred area that no one dared rob, people often left their valuables there for safekeeping.

Special public religious festivals also attracted people from the various city-states. Most of these, like the temples and shrines, were dedicated to specific gods. Often, great feasts or athletic competitions were held at these festivals. The most famous such competition, the Olympic Games, was dedicated to the god Zeus. These games were held at Olympia, located in the western part of the Peloponnesus, the large peninsula that makes up southern Greece. According to Robert Payne:

A foot race depicted on an amphora, or jar, from Attica. Dated about 530 B.C., the jar is two feet high.

Religious pilgrims offer gifts to the god Apollo at the Temple of Delphi.

The splendor of the festivals at Olympia outdid all other festivals. The *Hellenodikai*—the judges of the Hellenes—superintended the arrangements for the games, wearing robes of royal purple. Trumpeters announced the beginning of each race. . . . The foot race was always the first, but it was the chariot race that caused the greatest excitement, because it was the most dangerous. . . . Sometimes forty four-horsed chariots took part in the contest. . . . The chariot races were held in the morning. In the afternoon came the Pentathlon, a combined contest of running, jumping, wrestling, and throwing the javelin and discus. In the evening, under the golden moon, the

Young Spartan men at a gymnasium. A boxing match is in progress at lower left. Greek boxers continued to grapple even after one opponent was down.

victors marched in procession and sang hymns. . . [The victorious athletes were regarded with a reverence such as was given only to great military leaders. They were thought of as being in some special way more than human, almost godlike, for by acquiring honor in the games they had raised themselves above the common people.]

The Olympic Games took place every four years beginning in 776 B.C. These contests were so important to the Greeks that even during wartime, soldiers of enemy poleis laid down their arms and competed peacefully.

Prosperity Stimulates Change and Expansion

By the time of the first Olympics, Greece had completely recovered from its dark age. Trade, writing, architecture, and handicrafts had revived, and many poleis had become prosperous and powerful. Some of the most important poleis at this time were Athens; Thebes, located northwest of Athens; Corinth, Argos, and Sparta, all in the Peloponnesus; and Miletus, in Ionia on the coast of Asia Minor.

Greece's new prosperity stimulated these and other cities to expand and establish colonies. With the return of good times, local populations grew quickly and began consuming more food than could be grown locally or imported easily. Many of the poleis solved this problem by establishing colonies in more fertile areas and allowing portions of the home population to move there. For about two hundred years, the Greeks founded numerous colonies along the coasts of the Aegean, Mediterranean, and Black seas. Two of the most successful of these overseas poleis were Byzantium, located along the southern rim of the Black Sea, and Syracuse, on the western edge of the island of Sicily, directly south of Italy. So many prosperous Greek colonies sprang up in Italy that the

The First People in the World to Play

One of the qualities of the Greeks that distinguished them from other ancient peoples was their expression of the joy of life. This joy is evident in their art, sculpture, architecture, and literature. The renowned Greek scholar Edith Hamilton described how the Greeks lived life to its fullest. Said Hamilton in The Greek Way:

"While Egypt submitted and suffered and turned her face toward death, Greece resisted and rejoiced and turned full-face to life. For somewhere among those steep stone mountains, in little sheltered valleys where . . . men could have security for peace and happy living, something quite new came into the world; the joy of life found expression. Perhaps it was born there, among the shepherds pasturing their flocks where the wild flowers made a glory on the hillside; among the sailors on a sapphire sea washing enchanted islands. . . . The Greeks were the first people in the world to play, and they played on a great scale. All over Greece there were games . . . athletic contests of every description: races—horse-, boat-, torch-races; contests in music . . . in dancing . . . games where men leaped in and out of flying chariots; games so many one grows weary with the list of them. They are embodied in the statues familiar to all, the disc thrower, the charioteer, the wrestling boys, the dancing flute players. The great games—there were four that came at stated seasons—were so important, when one was held, a truce of God was proclaimed so that all Greece might come in safety without fear. . . . Splendor attended [an Olympic victor], processions, sacrifices, banquets, songs the greatest poets were glad to write. . . . If we had no other knowledge of what the Greeks were like, if nothing were left of Greek art and literature, the fact that they were in love with play and played magnificently would be proof enough of how they lived and how they looked at life. Wretched people, toiling people, do not play. Nothing like the Greek games is conceivable in Egypt. . . . And when Greece died . . . play, too, died out of the world. The brutal, bloody Roman games had nothing to do with the spirit of play. . . . Play died when Greece died and many a century passed before it was resurrected."

This engraving shows Athens as it appeared in the fifth century B.C.

region later became known in Latin as Magna Graecia, or "greater Greece."

Increased prosperity also helped bring about profound changes in the political structure of many Greek poleis. For centuries, the kings, who possessed most of the wealth, had ruled the cities. But as local economies thrived, some large landowners also grew wealthy. They banded together in groups, which eventually became powerful enough to overthrow the kings. By about 700 B.C., most Greek cities were ruled by groups consisting of several well-to-do aristocrats, a word derived from the Greek word *aristoi*, meaning "best people." This kind of government is called an oligarchy, which means "rule of the few" in Greek. The oligarchies were not very successful and often did not last long. Scholar Susan Peach explains:

> As trade increased, a middle class of merchants, craftsmen and bankers began to prosper. However, they could not take part in government, and soon began to demand a say in the decision making. Resentment of aristocratic power often led to riots. To re-establish

peace, people were sometimes prepared to allow one man to take absolute power. This sort of leader was called a tyrant.[13]

The modern meaning of the word *tyrant* is "a harsh ruler or dictator." Although some of the Greek tyrants did fit this description, many did not. Several were law-abiding, generous, and effective rulers. They often tried to maintain their popularity by sponsoring the arts and public building projects. One of the most successful tyrants was Peisistratus, who ruled Athens from 561 to 527 B.C. "Though he himself [was] an aristocrat," said C. M. Bowra, "he rose to power by promising to liberalize the land laws, and did so. . . . Peisistratus beautified the city, supported the art of poetry, encouraged drama and . . . commissioned [the writing of] a text of the *Iliad* and the *Odyssey*."[14]

A few city-states did not make the transition from kings to oligarchies and tyrants. The most important example was Sparta. The Spartans kept their kings and maintained a conservative, regimented society built around military training and the art of war. By the sixth century B.C., Sparta had the most powerful army in Greece and its soldiers were known for their skill and bravery. To maintain rigid discipline, the Spartans discouraged individual and artistic expression, so Sparta produced no significant art or literature. Unlike most other poleis, which were constantly instituting reforms, the Spartans distrusted change. They tried to have as little contact with outsiders as possible. Because Sparta's customs and attitudes were so different, rivalries and mutual distrust developed between the Spartans and their neighbors, especially the progressive Athenians.

In this view of ancient Sparta, the Eurotas River flows through the fore-ground and Mount Taygetos rises in the distance.

The Development of Democracy

But the Spartans were an exception. Many other cities heartily encouraged individualism and change. This had an important effect on the development of law and government in the seventh and sixth centuries B.C. Historian Victor Ehrenberg remarked:

> It was a period in which the individual for the first time found the means of expressing his or her personal feelings and experiences by writing lyric po-etry. . . . At the same time political in-dividualism developed out of the tensions of social life. . . . There was, on the one hand, the urgent demand of the ordinary peasants no longer to be the victims of the . . . [rule] of the aristocrats. . . . Oppression and injus-tice were causes of growing complaint,

and the first remedy was the codifica-tion [compiling] of law. . . . In various parts of the Greek world laws were written down for the first time. . . . Laws relating to the family, the rights of inheritance, and the position of slaves and foreigners were among the matters which increasingly became the concern of the state. . . . Hence even-tually sprang the idea . . . that the com-munity of the polis was based on the rule of law.[15]

Athens early took the lead in institut-ing laws and reforming its government. In 621 B.C., responding to the demands of the city's citizens, a political leader named Draco drew up a set of laws. Some of these were unusually harsh. For instance, if a debtor could not pay his creditor, the cred-itor could legally enslave the debtor. Even-tually, the people demanded that these laws be reformed.

In 594 B.C., a popular Athenian citizen named Solon became an archon, or an administrator who performed the everyday duties of government. The people, said Plutarch, "chose Solon to new-model and make laws. . . . First, then, he repealed all Draco's laws . . . because they were too severe, and the punishment too great."[16] Solon also set up a group of ordinary citizens called the Assembly to make laws and help choose rulers. This was an important step toward democracy, a word made up of the Greek words *demos,* meaning "people," and *kratos,* meaning "rule." A democratic government is one ruled by the people. The only major drawback to the Athenian system by modern standards was that only free males could be citizens and take part in government. Women, foreigners, and slaves were excluded. Since about one in

Solon Frees the Debtors

The Greeks remember the Athenian politician Solon as a wise and just leader who began revising the harsh laws that the earlier ruler, the tyrant Draco, had imposed. Under Draco, if a debtor could not repay a debt, the creditor could legally seize and enslave the debtor. The Greek historian Plutarch explained Solon's changes in his Lives, *the biographies of Greeks who shaped history. In canceling former debts, Solon created the forerunner of modern bankruptcy law:*

"As the moderns observe that the Athenians used to qualify the harshness of things by giving them softer and politer names, calling whores *mistresses,* tributes [bribes] *contributions,* garrisons *guards,* and prisons *castles,* so Solon seems to be the first who distinguished the canceling of debts by the name of *discharge.* For this was the first of his public acts, that debts should be forgiven and that no man in the future should take the body of his debtor for security. . . . For Solon ordered the minas [a money unit], which before went for but seventy-three drachmas, to go for a hundred so that, as they paid the same in value but much less in weight, those that had great sums to pay [debtors] were relieved while such as received them [creditors] were no losers. The greater part of writers, however, affirm that it was the abolition of past securities that was called a *discharge.* . . . He [Solon] prides himself on 'having taken away the marks of mortgaged land which before were almost everywhere set up and made free those fields which before were bound.' And not only this, but of such citizens as were seizable by their creditors for debt, some, he tells us, he had brought back from other countries [to] where they had [escaped] . . . and others he had set at liberty who had experienced a cruel slavery at home."

Property of
Bayport-Blue Point Public Library

A meeting of the Athenian Areopagus, a special council that advised city officials and acted as a criminal court. Council members held office for life.

three Athenians was a slave, and women and foreigners made up more than half of the remaining population, only about one in four people was a citizen.

Athens made the transition to complete democracy beginning in 508 B.C. under an enlightened ruler named Cleisthenes. He increased the importance of the Assembly, which met once every ten days. Every free male citizen had the right to speak out and vote in the Assembly. Cleisthenes also established the Council, a group of five hundred citizens who were chosen once a year by lot to make new laws and policies. These recommendations were then brought before the Assembly and debated and voted upon. Three archons and ten military leaders, called *strategoi*, elected once a year by the Assembly, ran the affairs of state and commanded the army.

Athens had taken a bold step. It had begun experimenting with concepts of freedom and self-rule that had never been tried before anywhere else in the world. Under their democratic system, the Athenians displayed a surge of energy and self-confidence that would soon lead them into an era of economic and cultural greatness.

Danger from the East

In the six hundred years following the breakdown of Mycenaean society, the Greeks built a rich, vibrant, and prosperous civilization. One reason that the city-states enjoyed such steady growth and development for so long was that no outside power hindered them. Large empires to the south and east of Greece, such as Egypt and Assyria, saw the tiny Greek cities as faraway and unimportant. So, for a long time, these great powers left the Greeks alone. But toward the end of the sixth century B.C., a new power rose in the east. The mighty Persian Empire expanded outward like a giant wave, destroying and absorbing every culture it encountered. That ominous wave now threatened to spread across the Aegean Sea, annihilate the Greeks, and engulf the rest of the Mediterranean world.

Chapter

3 West Versus East: The Greek and Persian Wars

During the years that many Greek cities were ruled by tyrants and democracy developed in Athens, the powerful Persian Empire rose in Asia. Persia originally occupied the area that is now Iran, east of the Persian Gulf. From there, Persian armies spread out in all directions and conquered every city and nation in their path. By the end of the sixth century B.C., the Persians controlled a vast territory that included Egypt, all of the Middle East, and Asia Minor. After defeating and absorbing the Greek cities of Ionia, Persia threatened to carry its aggression across the Aegean Sea to mainland Greece.

Many Greeks were convinced that Greece was doomed. Few thought that a handful of tiny Greek armies could match the huge Persian armies and reportedly invincible soldiers. Many people were so terrified of the Persians that they simply surrendered to them without a fight.

Facing the prospect of extinction, the Greeks realized that their only chance for survival was to unite. They must put aside old rivalries and join ranks against the common enemy. Some pointed out that they had done so once before, when their ancestors had crossed the Aegean and burned the towers of Troy. That legendary war over a single city had been but a small clash between West and East, between the cultures of Europe and Asia. In this new battle, the stakes were much higher. The fate of the entire Greek world was about to be decided.

Conquest and Rebellion

The Persian threat to Greece began in 546 B.C. when the Persian king Cyrus the Great conquered the Ionian cities along the coast of Asia Minor. The Persians forced the leaders of these Greek poleis to do the bidding of Persian governors called satraps. The Greeks also had to pay yearly tribute, large sums of money, acknowledging their submission to the Persians. Fearing for their own survival, the Greek cities on the mainland did little or nothing to help the Ionian poleis, and Cyrus maintained control over Ionia while he continued to expand his empire.

Later, in 521, Darius I became king of Persia. According to Herodotus, the Greek historian who later wrote a history of the Persian Wars, "Darius was an able and active monarch, ambitious to extend his power . . . into Europe."[17] Darius saw the Greeks as backward and weak but nevertheless an obstacle to the conquest of Europe. After removing that obstacle, he reasoned, it would be an easy matter to overrun the rest of Europe, then inhabited largely by scattered, tribal peoples even weaker than the Greeks.

In 512, Darius undertook the first phase of his European conquest by leading an army to the northern shore of the Aegean Sea and crossing the Hellespont. This narrow strait, now called the Dardanelles, separates Asia Minor from Europe. Darius conquered Thrace, a sparsely populated region of northern Greece, and some Aegean islands. He then returned to Persia, planning to continue his conquest later.

In 499, an event occurred that hastened Darius's return to Greece. Fed up with Persian rule, the Ionian cities, led by prosperous Miletus, revolted. They killed

Persia's Cyrus the Great, who captured the Greek Ionian cities in 546 B.C.

or expelled their Persian rulers, then attacked and burned the Persian city of Sardis in western Asia Minor. This time, two of the mainland poleis helped the Ionians. Athens and Eretria, located north of Athens on the island of Euboea, both sent ships and supplies to aid the revolt.

Darius's Revenge

The angry Darius brutally crushed the Ionian revolt. First, his navies defeated those of several Ionian cities. Not long afterward, he attacked Miletus, the richest and most beautiful city in Ionia. As Herodotus reported, the tragic fate of the Milesians caused widespread despair in Athens and other Greek mainland cities:

> The Persians, when they had vanquished the Ionians in the sea-fight, besieged Miletus both by land and sea, driving mines [tunnels] under the walls, and making use of every known device, until at length they took the whole town, six years from the time when the revolt first broke out.... All the inhabitants of the city they [killed or] reduced to slavery.... Those of the Milesians whose lives were spared ... were established [resettled] by him [Darius] in Ampe, a city on the shores of the Red Sea.... Miletus itself, and the plain about the city, were kept by the Persians for themselves.... The Athenians ... showed themselves beyond measure afflicted [distressed] at the fall of Miletus.... When ... [the poet Phrynichus] brought out upon the stage his drama, *The Capture of Miletus,* the whole theater burst into tears, and

Darius punished the other Ionian cities one by one, executing the leaders of the revolt and restoring Persian control. But quelling the Ionians alone was not enough to satisfy the king's desire for revenge. While he dealt with Ionia, Darius also began planning an invasion of the Greek mainland. He wanted not only to resume his conquest of Europe but also to punish the upstart Athenians and Eretrians for daring to interfere in Persian affairs. At the time of the revolt, recalled Herodotus, Darius wanted to know

> who, and what manner of men the Athenians were. And when he had been told, he called for his bow; and, having taken it, and placed an arrow on the string, he let the arrow fly toward heaven; and as he shot it into the air, he said, "Oh! Supreme God, grant me that I may avenge myself on the Athenians." And when he had said this, he appointed one of his servants to say to him every day as he sat at meat [supper], "Sire, remember the Athenians."[19]

Charge of the Hoplites

By 492, Darius had finished putting down the Ionian revolt and he turned his attention to Greece. He sent a fleet of ships commanded by his son-in-law Mardonius into the Aegean with orders to subdue Athens and Eretria. But a violent storm destroyed the fleet off the coast of Thrace. Two years later, Darius sent another expedition to Greece, this one led by a general named Datis and consisting of at least sixty thousand troops. First, the Persians landed

Persian king Darius I. Seen above protecting him is an image of the god Ahura Mazda, "the wise spirit."

the people sentenced him to pay a fine of a thousand drachmas [for depressing them]. They likewise made a law, that no one should ever again exhibit that piece.[18]

The Athenians and Plataeans drive the Persians to their ships in the battle of Marathon. Outnumbered by at least six to one, the Greeks won a decisive victory.

on Euboea, then burned Eretria and enslaved its inhabitants. Then, the invaders sailed to Marathon, on the coast of Attica some twenty-six miles northwest of Athens.

The news of the Persian assault sent a wave of fear through the Greek poleis. Athens appealed to other cities for help, especially Sparta. Though the two cities were traditional rivals, Athens desperately needed the skill and bravery of the Spartan soldiers. A runner named Phidippides carried the appeal to Sparta, covering the 150 miles in just two days. The Spartans agreed to send help but explained that they were in the midst of an important religious festival, and according to Spartan law, they could not leave until the festival was over.

Athens realized it had to face the enemy alone. A force of nine thousand Athenian troops marched overland to Marathon and camped near the flat, open plain on which the Persians had disembarked. There, about one thousand men, the entire army of the nearby tiny polis of Plataea, a longtime ally of Athens, joined the Athenians.

The Greeks, vastly outnumbered, realized that their fate, and perhaps the fate of all Greece, now depended on their courage and skill in the coming battle. Their effectiveness against the reported ferocity of the Persians had not yet been tested. But the Greeks had confidence in their own weaponry and training. Historian Archer Jones explained:

The Greeks fought on foot, hand-to-hand, with spear and sword, in a form of fighting known as shock action. The Greek soldiers, called hoplites, naturally protected themselves with shields, helmets, and breastplates, and covered other parts of the body as well. This usually metal armor, together with sword and spear, constituted a substantial burden, which made running difficult, and gave these soldiers their name,

The Athenians Charge at Dawn

Most historians consider the battle of Marathon in 490 B.C. one of the most decisive battles in history. The crushing defeat the Athenians delivered to the invading troops of King Darius at Marathon forever destroyed the myth of Persian superiority. Historians Joseph B. Mitchell and Sir Edward Creasy tell how, despite the formidable odds, the Greeks decided to take the offensive and attack at dawn:

"They saw before them the invading forces of a mighty empire that in the last fifty years had shattered and enslaved all the kingdoms . . . of the then known world. . . . According to old national custom the warriors of each [Greek] tribe were arrayed together. Neighbor thus fought beside neighbor, friend by friend . . . The trumpet sounded for action; the little army bore down upon the host of the foe. Instead of advancing at the usual slow pace of the phalanx [the troop formation], Callimachus brought his men on at double time. It was of the greatest importance to achieve the utmost in surprise, to cross as rapidly as possible the mile or so of level ground that lay between the foot of the mountain and the Persian forces, before the enemy's generals could deploy their masses in line. . . . On came the Greeks with one unwavering line of leveled spears, and struck the rapidly forming Persian line. The front rank of the Asiatics [went] down to a man at the first shock. . . . On the wings the Greeks quickly routed the enemy opposing them, but in the center . . . the Persians . . . drove the Athenians back. . . . At a trumpet signal the two victorious Greek wings wheeled inward and struck both flanks of the advancing Persians. Meanwhile the Greek center rallied and renewed the struggle. . . . The foremost Persians kept rushing forward upon the projecting spears of the Greeks. . . . At last the Persians broke and fled; the Greeks followed in pursuit to the water's edge, where the invaders sought to launch their galleys. The Athenians attacked and sought to set fire to the fleet. . . . Here fell the brave War Ruler Callimachus. Seven galleys were secured [by the Greeks]; but the Persians succeeded in saving the rest. . . . The number of Persians dead was . . . 6,400. The Athenian loss was . . . 192."

Athenian general Miltiades leads the charge against the Persians at Marathon.

heavy infantry. The completeness and quality of their equipment made up the only professional attributes of the Greek hoplites. Militiamen, they had full-time occupations as farmers, artisans, and tradesmen, furnished their own armor, had engaged in some training, and tried to keep in good physical condition. . . . Before the combat, the hoplite commander usually addressed them to raise their confidence and courage.[20]

On the night before the battle, the Greeks at Marathon listened to just such a morale-boosting speech from their commander, Miltiades, one of the ten elected generals of Athens. The future of Greece, he told them, was in their hands.

At dawn on September 12, 490, the hoplites formed ranks and at a trumpet signal charged at a run across the plain toward the Persians. The Persians were astounded when they saw the Greeks advancing and heard their loud war cries. Herodotus said, "The barbarians thought the Athenians were mad, rushing to their own destruc-

tion, for there were so few of them and yet they were charging on the run, without the support of cavalry [horsemen] or archers."[21]

Minutes later, the Greeks, their spears and swords raised to strike, smashed with devastating force into the enemy lines. The front ranks of Darius's army reeled from the blow as hundreds of Persians fell dead in the first few seconds of combat. The Greeks then began a bloody slaughter that lasted for several hours. The heavily armed hoplites proved vastly superior to the Persian soldiers, who wore little armor and were not as well trained in shock combat. Eventually, the Persians, confused and afraid, broke ranks and fled for their ships. The Greeks followed, capturing seven of the vessels before the rest managed to escape. More than 6,400 Persian bodies littered the battlefield, while the Greeks lost only 192 men. The Greeks had forever shattered the myth of Persian invincibility.

Athens Triumphant

Immediately after the battle, Miltiades dispatched Phidippides, recently back from his Spartan mission, to Athens to announce the victory. Despite his fatigue after fighting in the grueling battle, the runner managed to cover the twenty-six miles in a few hours. Reaching Athens, he delivered his message and fell dead of exhaustion. Centuries later, the modern Olympics introduced a "marathon" race of twenty-six miles in honor of Phidippides' feat of strength and valor.

After escaping Marathon, the Persians sailed around Attica with the intention of attacking Athens. Anticipating this move, the Greek army marched at an exhausting pace back to the city. When the Persians arrived, they found the very same warriors who had just defeated them lined up and ready to fight another battle. Prudently, the Persians retreated and sailed back to Persia.

All of the Greek poleis celebrated the astonishing Athenian victory, and the hoplites of Marathon became national heroes. Historian Peter Levi said:

> Memorials in marble and bronze [built] at Marathon and Delphi can hardly express the Athenian triumph. There were poems, a famous painting, legends and written histories. Six hundred and fifty years later, travelers still believed they heard ghostly noises of armed men when they crossed the battlefield. Those who fought at Marathon were known as the "men of Marathon" for the rest of their lives.[22]

As the acknowledged savior of Greece, Athens gained much prestige, and in the following few years, it grew increasingly prosperous. It began new public building projects, including a temple on its central hill, the Acropolis. The Athenians dedicated this temple, called the Parthenon, to the city's patron deity—Athena, goddess of wisdom and war.

The Athenians also expanded their democracy. Among other reforms, they instituted the system of ostracism, designed to prevent tyrants or unpopular rulers from remaining in power. Once a year, during ostracism, the citizens met in the marketplace, or *agora*. Each wrote the name of a politician he wished to get rid of on a piece of broken pottery called an *ostrakon*. If a leader received more than six thousand of these negative votes, the city banished him for ten years.

A reconstruction of Phidias's 40-foot-high statue of Athena which stood inside the Parthenon.

A Savage Fight to the Death

While Athens celebrated and prospered, Darius, who now hated the Athenians more than ever, prepared to launch still another invasion of Greece. But he died in 485 B.C. without achieving his revenge. Succeeding to the Persian throne, Darius's son Xerxes was determined to resume his father's conquest of Europe. In 480, Xerxes led a huge force, as many as 200,000 troops and one thousand ships, across the Hellespont. The Persians marched southward through Thrace and Thessaly, burning and pillaging most of the Greek poleis along the way. Xerxes' plan was to enter southern Greece through the pass of Thermopylae, in the mountains west of Euboea, then attack Athens and other cities.

The Greeks decided that their best hope of halting the Persian advance was to make a stand at Thermopylae, which was very narrow. Herodotus explained, "At one point the mountain and sea came so close together that the ground along the shore was only fifty feet wide. . . . This was the place at which the Greeks . . . thought they could resist the Persians successfully; for in this small space the enormous size of the Persian army would be of no advantage."[23] A united Greek army of about seven thousand men from poleis including Arcadia, Mantinea, Corinth, Thespiae, and Phocis fortified the pass. They were led by Leonidas, king of Sparta, and three hundred handpicked Spartan hoplites.

The Greeks at Thermopylae watched grimly as the enormous Persian horde drew near. For two days, the Persians attacked at intervals but could make no headway against the Greeks, who once more demonstrated their superiority over

Facing impossible odds, the Greeks fight to the death in the narrow pass of Thermopylae.

Persian troops. Then, a Greek traitor led a contingent of Persians along a little-known mountain path toward the Greeks' rear. Realizing that the Greek position soon would be hopeless, Leonidas ordered the bulk of the army to withdraw. He and his three hundred Spartans, along with a few hundred men from other poleis, remained, determined to fight to the death.

Shaded from the sun by an attendant, Persia's king Xerxes gives an audience.

Total Victory

Xerxes now marched his gigantic army southward unopposed. On September 17, 480, the Persians entered Athens but found the city empty. The entire population had evacuated to nearby islands. The Persian king burned the Parthenon and other buildings on the Acropolis, confident that he had finally avenged the wrongs the Athenians had done him and his father.

But Xerxes' triumph was short-lived. While the heroes of Thermopylae had delayed the Persians, other Greeks had been busy readying warships to attack the huge Persian fleet. The Athenian admiral Themistocles assumed charge of the Greek fleet of fewer than three hundred ships. He positioned them in the narrow straits of Salamis, a few miles south of Athens, and waited for the Persians to attack.

Three days after Xerxes sacked Athens, he ordered his entire fleet into the straits of Salamis with orders to destroy all of the Greek ships. But the Greek galleys were smaller and more maneuverable than the heavy Persian vessels. The Greeks darted in and out, inflicting heavy damage on the helpless Persians. "Most of the Persian vessels were lost," wrote Herodotus, "when their ships in the front rank were beaten, and turned to flee, for the commanders of the ships in the rear continued to press forward. . . . So the ships coming forward and the ships retreating got in each other's way."[25] The Persian sailors died by the thousands. The Greek playwright Aeschylus, who fought at Salamis, later described the massacre in his play *The Persians:*

A savage battle followed, in which the tiny band of Greeks boldly abandoned their defensive position and attacked. The Persians fell in heaps as the hoplites cut their way through the enemy lines. Eventually, the other Persians closed in from the rear. According to Herodotus, when the Greeks found themselves surrounded, they

> stationed themselves on the little hill in the entrance to the pass. . . . Here they defended themselves with their swords, as long as they had them, and then with fists and teeth, until the foreigners overwhelmed them and struck them down. Some foreigners attacked them from the front . . . others came from behind, all taking their stand around them in a ring. Such was the bravery of the Spartans.[24]

After the battle, Xerxes counted his losses. A mere handful of men had killed more than twenty thousand Persians. The king was so enraged that he ordered his men to cut off Leonidas's head and mount it on a pole for all his soldiers to see.

Athenian crowds joyously celebrate on the beaches following the Greeks' crushing defeat of the Persian fleet at Salamis.

The sea vanished
Under a clogged carpet of
  shipwrecks, limbs, torsos,
No sea, and the beaches were
  cluttered with the dead,
And the rocks in the bay were
  cluttered,
The Asian ships whirling about
  in an insane rout,
While with snapped oars, balks
  of timber from wreckage,
The Greeks stoved [crushed] and
  hammered and slew.[26]

The Persians lost more than two hundred ships, with hundreds more damaged, while the Greeks lost only forty ships. Angry and frustrated, Xerxes sailed the rest of his vessels away to Asia Minor.

Despite this damaging defeat, Xerxes refused to give up the conquest of Greece. He left behind 150,000 troops under Mardonius to carry on the war. The following summer, in August 479, men from dozens of different poleis converged on the Persians near Plataea. There, the largest united Greek army yet assembled, some 100,000

hoplites, annihilated Mardonius's army. On the same day, near Mycale on the coast of Asia Minor, Greek warships destroyed the Persian fleet that Xerxes had left behind to control Ionia. The Ionian Greeks were free once more.

The unexpected Greek victory in the war assured continued freedom for all of the Greeks. The victory was also one of the most decisive events in world history because it kept the Persians from conquering Europe. In fact, Will Durant remarked, the Greek defeat of Persia "made Europe possible. It won for Western civilization the opportunity to develop its own economic life . . . its own political institutions."[27] The victory also filled the Greeks with pride. They had demonstrated to the world and to themselves that they, like their ancestors at Troy, were capable of glorious achievements. The victory, said historian W. G. Hardy, "was the torch to set fire to the brilliance of the great age of the Greeks. There was a tremendous upswelling of confidence . . . [and now] the Greeks felt there was nothing they could not attempt."[28]

Chapter

4 Athenian Empire: Power and Expansion Inflame Old Rivalries

The defeat of Persia did more than save Greece from foreign oppression. It also solidified and increased the power of both Athens and Sparta. Although many Greek poleis had taken part in the patriotic war, Athens and Sparta were the leaders. This was only natural, since Athens had the most powerful navy in Greece and Sparta had the strongest army. Yet the victory, engineered mainly by Athenian and Spartan generals, had been larger and more stunning than anyone could have predicted. This significantly increased the prestige and influence of these two cities. "These were now the two leading powers [in

Warships like these, seen defeating the Persians at Salamis, were the backbone of the powerful Athenian navy.

Greece]," wrote the Greek historian Thucydides, "the one strong by land and the other by sea."[29]

Trouble between these two powerful cities was inevitable, however. They could not find ways of settling their many differences. The Persian threat had only temporarily persuaded them to put aside their long-standing mutual distrust. After the Persian defeat, the two cities quickly reverted to their traditional rivalry, and relations between them steadily deteriorated. The Spartans watched in dismay as Athens rapidly utilized its new wealth and power to build itself a prosperous empire and expand its democracy. Athens's constant struggle to increase its power and influence and Sparta's attempts to curb that influence would dominate the affairs of the Greek world during the following century.

Mutual Fears of Aggression

The rivalry between Athens and Sparta was based mainly on political differences and mutual fears of military aggression. The Athenians, proud of their new democracy, wanted to spread the ideals of freedom and self-rule to other poleis. They saw Spartan rule by kings and aristocrats as an

The dromos, *or public walkway, of ancient Sparta. On the pedestals in front of the semicircular sitting area stand statues of the gods Castor and Pollux.*

old-fashioned and inferior system. The Athenians worried that the Spartans might one day use their powerful army to force this inferior system on Athens and other poleis. On the other hand, the Spartans believed their own system to be superior and saw Athenian democratic ideals as a dangerous threat to Sparta's established order. The Spartans worried that Athens might convince Sparta's neighbors in the Peloponnesus to become democracies. This, the Spartans believed, would weaken their own dominant influence in the region. The Spartans also feared that the increasing prosperity of the Athenians might eventually enable them to attack and destroy Sparta. "The growth of Athenian power," stated Thucydides, "terrified the Spartans and put them under the necessity of fighting."[30]

Despite the much-feared strength of Sparta's army, in the first few decades fol-

lowing the Persian Wars, the Spartans did not vigorously or effectively oppose the Athenians. This was partly because the Spartans were preoccupied with a number of internal troubles during these years. But Sparta's lack of action also stemmed from a major difference in attitude between the two peoples. The Athenians were adventurous and tended to take risks, such as pouring most of their resources into developing their fleets. That risk paid off, giving the city control of the seas and the riches and prosperity earned from widespread trade and commerce.

By contrast, the Spartans, who had always been reluctant sailors, preferred to stay near home, work their farms, and maintain their traditional, conservative ways. As a result, they were unable to achieve the economic strength of the Athenians. The Spartan lack of initiative was well known and often criticized by other

The Fleet—Backbone of the Empire

After the Persian Wars, Athens, located in the region called Attica, rapidly expanded its influence over the Aegean islands and other parts of the Mediterranean through trade. In his classic work Ancient Times: A History of the Early World, *historian James Henry Breasted described how Corinth and the island of Aegina, both near Athens, were the first Greek seaports to become prosperous after the wars:*

"They were at once followed, however, by the little harbor town of Piraeus, built by the foresight of Themistocles as the port of Athens. Along its busy docks were moored Greek ships from all over the Mediterranean world, for the defeat of the Phoenicians [a people from the Middle East who had earlier controlled sea trade] in east and west had broken up their merchant fleets and thrown much of their trade into the hands of the Greeks. Here many a Greek ship from the Black Sea, laden with grain or fish, moored alongside the grain ships of Egypt, and the mixed cargoes from Syracuse [in Sicily]; for Attica was no longer producing food enough for her own need, and it was necessary to import it. The docks were piled high with goods from the Athenian factories, and long lines of perspiring porters were loading them into ships bound for all the harbors of the Mediterranean. Scores of battleships stretched far along the shores, and the busy shipyards and dry docks, filled with multitudes of workmen, were noisy with the sound of many hammers. In spite of much progress in navigation we must not think of these ancient ships of Greece as very large. A merchant vessel carrying from two hundred and fifty to three hundred tons was considered large in Fifth-Century Greece. Ships clung timidly to the shore and rarely ventured to sea in the stormy winter season. They had no compass or charts, there were no lighthouses, and they were often plundered by pirates. . . . On the other hand, the profits gained from sea-borne commerce might be very considerable. A vessel that reached the north shores of the Black Sea . . . might sell its cargo so profitably as to bring back to the owner double the first cost of the goods after paying all expenses."

Greeks. For instance, ambassadors from Corinth, who also worried about Athens's growing power, told Spartan leaders:

> You have never fully considered what manner of men these Athenians are. . . . They are innovators, equally quick in the conception and in the execution of every plan; while you are careful only to keep what you have and [are] uninventive. . . . They are audacious [bold] beyond their strength; they run risks which policy would condemn; and in the midst of dangers, they are full of hope. Whereas it is your nature to act more feebly than your power allows. . . . They are resolute [determined], and you are dilatory [slow acting]; they are always abroad, and you are always home.[31]

The Delian League

Sparta's inaction left Athens largely free to expand its power and influence, which it did quickly and on a grand scale. Between 479 and 457 B.C., Athens built an empire that dominated large sections of the Mediterranean world. At first, the city gained much of its wealth, prestige, and power by continuing its leadership against Persia. Although the Greeks had soundly defeated the Persians, the Persian Empire, the largest in the world at the time, was still intact. Many Greeks believed that the Persians might one day reorganize and attempt another invasion of the Greek mainland. And Persian strongholds in Asia Minor posed a constant threat to the freedom of the Greek cities of Ionia. The

Greeks had been successful against the Persians by banding together. Athens now proposed to continue that success by forming a major Greek alliance. Sparta and its neighbors, who disagreed that the Persians were still a threat and who hated the Athenians, refused to join.

So, in 477, delegates from Athens, the Ionian cities, and most of the Aegean islands met on the island of Delos. They established an alliance called the Delian League, with the purpose of protecting Greece from further Persian aggression. Each member of the league agreed to contribute ships, money, or both to defensive and offensive actions against the Persians. According to Thucydides, because Athens was the strongest member, "the Athenians took over the leadership [of the league] by a voluntary act of the allies." The Athenians, wrote Thucydides, "fixed which of the cities should supply money and which ships for the war against the barbarians. . . . The island of Delos was the [league] treasury, and the councils [meetings] of the allies were held there in the temple."[32] As the league's leader, Athens acquired many political allies and a great deal of prestige and military power.

The allied forces of the Delian League swiftly went into action. First, they swept through the Aegean, rooting out and punishing any Greeks who had aided the enemy during the Persian Wars. Next, the league members decided to avenge the Persian invasion itself by launching an offensive against Persian cities in Asia Minor. Between 476 and 469, the armies of the Delian League engaged in a bloody campaign against the Persians. The Greeks were led by a skilled Athenian general named Cimon, son of Miltiades, the hero of Marathon.

Cimon Expands Athenian Power

While Cimon commanded Athens's overseas army, Themistocles, still popular after his victory at Salamis, dominated Athenian affairs in Attica. Themistocles built more ships and expanded and strengthened the port city of Piraeus, enhancing Athenian trade capabilities. He also constructed massive defensive walls around Athens, a barrier strong enough to keep any enemy from entering the city.

But Themistocles' popularity did not last long. About the year 472, the Athenians ostracized him, supposedly for taking bribes, and Cimon became Athens's most

Cimon's good looks and long curly hair, described by Plutarch, are captured by a Roman artist.

This Roman depiction of Themistocles pictures him without the full beard customary in his time.

popular and powerful leader. According to Plutarch, all facets of Cimon's character

> were noble and good. He was daring as Miltiades, and not inferior to Themistocles in judgment, and was incomparably more just and honest than either of them. . . . He was also of a fairly handsome person . . . tall and large, and let his thick and curly hair grow long. . . . He obtained great repute [popularity] among the Athenians, and was regarded with affection, as well as admiration.[33]

In 469, Cimon gained further popularity by commanding the forces of the Delian League in a crushing defeat of the Persians near the southern coast of Asia Minor.

Desiring to increase Athens's prosperity, Cimon took full advantage of the city's position as leader of the Delian League. He began treating the other league members less like allies and more like Athenian subjects, requiring new cities joining the alliance to swear to the following oath: "I will not revolt from the people of the Athenians in any way or shape, in word or deed, or be an accomplice in revolt. . . . I will pay the Athenians the tribute [money for the league treasury], and I will be a faithful and true ally to the utmost of my power. I will help and assist the Athenian people if anyone injures them; and I will obey their commands."[34]

Cimon used Athens's powerful fleet to intimidate and control the other league members. That way, as the league expanded and acquired more trading partners, Athens's influence, wealth, and prestige also expanded. "The Athenians were exacting and oppressive [harsh]," wrote Thucydides,

> using coercive measures [threats and military force] toward men who were neither willing nor accustomed to work hard. . . . They [the Athenians] no longer fought upon an equality with the rest of the confederates [allies], and they had no difficulty in reducing [defeating] them when they revolted. . . . The Athenians acquired a firmer hold over their empire, and the city itself became a great power.[35]

Sparta was extremely jealous of Athens's success. But even when the Spartans overcame their usual reluctance to take action, they could do little to check Athenian expansion. Between 478 and 464, a series of political and natural disasters struck Sparta. First, some Spartan leaders, who had earlier won praise as heroes in the Persian Wars, began collaborating with the Persians. This caused Sparta a major loss of prestige and pushed many poleis into the Athenian sphere of in-

fluence. In the 470s, Argos, Elis, and Mantinea, all Sparta's neighbors in the Peloponnesus, dismantled their oligarchies and instituted Athenian-style democracies. Then, in 464, a huge earthquake struck Sparta, leveling most of its buildings. Taking advantage of the confusion that followed, the Spartan slaves, called helots, rebelled. It took the Spartans five years to put down the uprising and even longer to rebuild their ruined city.

The Aegean Becomes an Athenian Lake

While Sparta dealt with its troubles, Athens continued to extend its influence. Athens had grown rich, partly through trade but also because of the flow of silver from its mines near Mount Laurium in southern Attica. The city's domination of the Delian League also increased its wealth. The money from the league's treasury at Delos, once used to finance expeditions against Persia, was now largely at Athens's disposal. The city used much of its wealth to establish new Athenian colonies all around the Mediterranean. The empire that Athens had created in less than thirty years, said W. G. Hardy,

> had only about three million souls in it. But it was, for the Greek world, a big one. There were ultimately . . . about 250 communities, each bound to Athens by separate political and commercial treaties. The Aegean was an Athenian lake. Athenian warships guarded the entrance to the Black Sea and Athenian soldiers served in the islands, in Macedonia [in northern Greece], and in Asia Minor. Fat-bellied

merchantmen [cargo ships] brought to Piraeus linen and papyrus [writing parchment] from Egypt, frankincense [spice] from Syria, dates and wheat flour from Phoenicia, pork and cheese from Syracuse, ivory from Africa, hides and cheeses from Gaul [France] . . . iron ore from Elba [a Mediterranean island], and the wheat of the Ukraine [the land north of the Black Sea].[36]

One reason that Athens's empire thrived was that the city minted its own valuable silver coins, called drachmas. These were also called "owls" because they bore an image of an owl, the symbol of the goddess Athena. Athenian drachmas soon became the common currency of the Mediterranean world, helping to bind Athens's colonies and trading partners to the mother city.

The Rise of Pericles

Although much of Athens's success had been the result of Cimon's strong leadership of both the city and the Delian League, some Athenians resented him. He had often stated his desire to make friends with the Spartans, believing that cooperation between the two cities would be beneficial for all Greeks. He had even offered to send Athenian troops to help the Spartans put down the helot rebellion. In 461, Cimon's political opponents successfully took advantage of his "pro-Spartan" position and accused him of siding with the Spartans against the Athenian people. Cimon was ostracized and banished.

One of Cimon's opponents, a young man named Pericles, swiftly gained the confidence of the people and became the most powerful political leader in Athens. Pericles was a wise, educated, fair, and enlightened statesman as well as an inspiring orator. Under his leadership, which lasted for thirty years, Athens reached new heights of power, influence, and cultural achievement. "Great as Athens had been when he became her leader," said Plutarch, "he made her the greatest of all cities, and he came to hold more power in his hands than many a king or tyrant."[37]

Pericles realized that for Athens to maintain its power and prosperity, it must be safe from attack. He convinced his fellow

Because his head was shaped abnormally, Pericles insisted that sculptors always show him wearing a helmet.

First Citizen of Athens

As leader of Athens during its golden age, Pericles is remembered as one of history's great leaders. In his Lives, *the Greek writer Plutarch described some of the background and admirable character traits of Athens's first citizen:*

"His family was one of the most considerable in Athens, both on his father's and mother's side. . . . His person in other respects was well-turned [handsome], but his head was disproportionately long. For this reason almost all his statues have the head covered with a helmet, the sculptors choosing, I suppose, to hide the defect. The Athenian poets called him *Schinocephalos,* or Onion-Head. . . . The philosopher [teacher] with whom he was most intimately acquainted, who gave him that force and sublimity of sentiment [depth of emotion and expression] . . . who, in short, formed him to that admirable dignity of manners, was Anaxagoras. . . . Charmed with the company of this philosopher . . . Pericles acquired not only . . . a loftiness and purity of style [dignified and clear way of expression] far removed from the low expression of the vulgar, but likewise a gravity of countenance [serious attitude] which relaxed not into laughter, a firm and even tone of voice, an easy deportment [pleasant manners], and a decency of dress which no vehemence of speaking ever put into disorder [no one could find fault with]. These things, and others of a like nature, excited admiration in all who saw him. Such was his conduct that, when a vile and abandoned fellow [derelict] loaded him all day with reproaches and abuse [harassed him], he bore it with patience and silence and continued in public to dispatch some urgent affairs [went about his business]. In the evening he walked softly home, this impudent wretch following, insulting him all the way with the most scurrilous [obscene] language. As it was dark when Pericles came to his own door, he ordered one of his servants to take a torch and light the man home."

Athens's port of Piraeus, with the Long Walls stretching away toward the city.

citizens that the walls built by Themistocles were not an adequate defense. Since Athens was not directly on the sea, an attacking army could camp outside the walls and starve the city into submission. So Pericles ordered the construction of the Long Walls, stretching nearly five miles from Athens to its harbor, Piraeus. Now, if an enemy threatened, the Athenians could move the population of Attica inside the walls. As long as Athens's fleet controlled the seas, Pericles believed, the city could get fresh supplies of food and outlast any siege.

The Wonder of Future Ages

Pericles, a champion of democracy, believed that his city's government should be as strong as its defenses. So, while building the Long Walls, which were completed in 458 B.C., he also began strengthening the democracy. His most important reform was the introduction of payment for government service. According to Robert Payne:

Cleisthenes had introduced a form of democratic government which established equality by making all, or nearly all, the offices of state open to the people chosen by lot, thus ensuring that everyone had an opportunity to serve the state. . . . Pericles observed the flaw in the argument. The shoemaker . . . and the schoolteacher could serve the state only if they had private incomes or could somehow arrange for others to take over their duties while they were serving on the state boards. The rich could afford to serve . . . the poor could not. Pericles therefore instituted a system of payment from the state treasury for all government servants. The poorest citizens were now able to serve, without the fear of living in official poverty.[38]

Like most Athenians, Pericles took great pride in Athens's democracy. He believed that its ideals of freedom and individual expression made the polis and its government strong and flexible. He said:

Our constitution is called a democracy because power is in the hands not of a minority but of the whole people. When it is a question of settling private disputes, everyone is equal before the law; when it is a question of putting one person before another in positions of public responsibility, what counts is not membership of a particular class, but the actual ability which the man possesses. . . . Here, each individual is interested not only in his own affairs, but in the affairs of the state as well . . . we do not say that a man who takes no interest in politics is a man who minds his own business; we say that he has no business here at all.[39]

Hair Dyes and Freckle Removers

Thanks to commentary in plays and other writings of classical Greece that have survived to the present, much is known about the appearance and personal habits of the Greeks. In the following description by historian Will Durant, the daily grooming and hygiene habits of the Greeks of twenty-five centuries ago seem just as varied, detailed, and important as those of today:

"The citizens of Athens, in the fifth century, are men of medium height, vigorous, bearded. . . . Greek women, like others [in later ages], find their figures a little short of perfection. They lengthen them with high cork soles on their shoes, pad out deficiencies with wadding [stuffing], compress abundances [fat areas] with lacing, and support the breasts with a cloth brassiere. The hair of the Greeks is usually dark; blondes are exceptional, and much admired; many women, and some men, dye their hair to make it blonde, or to conceal the grayness of age. Both sexes use oils to help the growth of the hair and to protect it against the sun; the women, and again some of the men, add perfumes to the oil. Both sexes . . . wear the hair long, usually bound in braids around or behind the head. . . . The women vary their coiffure by knotting the hair low on the nape of the neck, or letting it fall over the shoulders, or around the neck and upon the breast. The ladies like to bind their hair with gay ribbons, and to adorn these with a jewel on the forehead. . . . No Greek [man] ever wears a mustache without a beard. The beard is neatly trimmed, usually to a point. The barber not only cuts the hair and shaves or trims the beard, but he manicures his customer and otherwise polishes him up for presentation; when he has finished he offers him a mirror in the most modern style. . . . The women also shave here and there, using razors or depilatories [hair removers] of arsenic and lime. Perfumes—made from flowers, with a base of oil—are numbered in the hundreds; Socrates complains that men make so much use of them. Every lady of class has an armory of mirrors, pins, hairpins, safety pins, tweezers, combs, scent bottles, and pots for rouge and creams. Cheeks and lips are painted with sticks of minium or alkanet root . . . eyelashes are darkened, and then set with a mixture of egg white and gum ammoniac. Creams and washes are used for removing wrinkles, freckles, and spots."

Pericles also tapped the power of individual expression in Athens by vigorously promoting building projects, the arts, and literature. Using money from the Delian League treasury, he beautified the city and rebuilt the temples on the Acropolis that had been destroyed by the Persians. He encouraged the work of dramatists, painters, sculptors, and scientists. His goal was to make Athens a model city, not only for his own time but for all times to come. "Future ages will wonder at us," he correctly predicted, "as the present age wonders at us now."[40]

This frieze from the Parthenon on the Athenian Acropolis shows the painstaking detail and artistry of the Athenians.

Trying to Do Too Much at Once

But at the height of its success, Athens began to encounter some serious problems. First, Sparta had recovered from its internal troubles by 457 B.C., and it began using its power and influence to oppose Athens. Over the course of the next two decades, Athens fought a number of small but bloody and expensive wars with neighboring cities, among them Corinth, Aegina, and Thebes. Hoping to help defeat Athens, Sparta allied itself with these cities and provided them with military backing. Athens held its own in these conflicts, but they badly drained its resources and energy.

Athens also experienced some disastrous military and political setbacks. In 461, the Egyptians rebelled against Persian rule and asked for Athenian aid. Athens sent a large military force to help the Egyptians but lost most of the men and ships in a major defeat in 454. To make matters worse, in the 440s, several poleis controlled by Athens, including Boeotia, Megara, and Euboea, rebelled. Some cities cast off their Athenian-style democracies and brought back oligarchies. Athens was unable to quell all of these rebellions, and some of its former allies signed treaties with Sparta.

Most of these problems occurred because Athens, in its constant attempt to expand its power and influence, had overextended itself. Despite its vast wealth, prestige, and human resources, it could not effectively sustain and control the ambitious empire it had created. This weakness would have serious consequences later. It would allow Sparta to challenge Athens for supremacy in Greece. Eventually, the two powers would confront each other in a devastating conflict that would affect the entire Greek world.

Chapter 5

Cultural Outburst: The Golden Age of Athens

The period from 479 to 431 B.C. is often referred to as Athens's golden age. During these years, while the city built its empire, Athenian leaders, especially Pericles, sought to make it a model for all other cities. The government actively encouraged cultural activities of all kinds. Athenian art, sculpture, architecture, philosophy, science, and drama flourished and quickly reached heights of expression never before seen in human history. This cultural outburst produced a magnificent artistic and literary legacy that has awed and inspired the world ever since.

The Athenians were able to achieve so much in so short a time because their city enjoyed a unique set of circumstances. First, a vast trade network made Athenians aware of the products, customs, and arts of

Athenian vases of various styles and periods. From left to right: ancient, funeral, perfected, and intermediate.

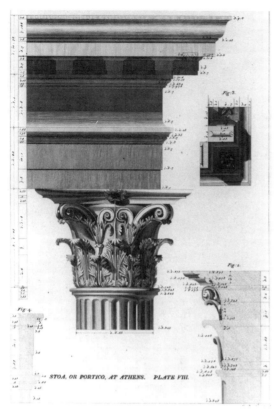

An architectural illustration shows how a Greek Corinthian column supports the architrave, a horizontal beam, which, in turn, supports the ornamental cornice.

strange and distant peoples. The constant influx of new goods and ideas made Athens a very cosmopolitan, or worldly, city. Also, the city accumulated a great deal of wealth from trade and from its silver mines. The government poured much of this money into elaborate festivals and huge public building projects that no other city at the time could afford to match. In addition, the city's democratic institutions encouraged individual expression. Because of these factors, Athens attained the image of a modern, progressive, and tolerant city, and it attracted artists

and intellectuals from many other cities and countries. Athens achieved cultural greatness because the money and atmosphere it provided encouraged creative people to express themselves.

Craftsmen and Slaves

Most of the artists, builders, and writers that made Athens great were free males who were citizens because they were born in the city. But members of other social groups, including free males without citizenship, women, and slaves, also contributed indirectly to the city's greatness. Without the labor and support of these groups, the creative artists could not have achieved what they did.

Vase showing a bootmaker, at left, cutting the leather for a lady's shoe.

Euripides, the Athenian playwright, of whose ninety-two plays only eighteen have survived.

Free males who were not allowed to become citizens because they were born in foreign cities or countries were called *metics*. They were usually traders and craftsmen who came to live and work in Athens. Although they could not take part in the government, many metics became important and prosperous members of the community. They provided many vital services, including operating food markets and making shoes, pottery, and jewelry. And the metics who practiced metal smithing, toolmaking, and stone masonry made the great works of the sculptors and architects possible.

The work of the architects and builders, as well as that of most other free Athenians, was also supported by slave labor. Slaves were usually foreigners captured in wars or bought in foreign slave markets. It is estimated that of Athens's

population of about 270,000 in the golden age, some 80,000 were slaves. A few citizens considered the idea of one person owning another to be wrong. The playwright Euripides, for example, wrote, "Slavery, that thing of evil, by its nature evil, forcing submission from man to what no man should yield to."[41] However, most Athenians, like other people in the ancient world, accepted slavery as a natural and necessary institution. The Athenian slaves did most of the difficult labor in the mines, in building projects, and in the home.

Yet, unlike slave owners in other places and times, the Athenians, for the most part, treated their slaves well. The law even protected slaves against abuse, said historian C. E. Robinson.

> It was not permitted to put a slave to death. . . . Slaves at Athens were anything but cringing creatures. They would even elbow passers-by out of their way in the street; and . . . it was unsafe to punch their heads; for in dress and appearance they were so like the free-born citizens that it was quite easy to make a mistake. In the home they were frequently accepted almost as one of the family. Many were given skillful and responsible jobs. . . . They were even given wages and allowed to accumulate savings, with the prospect that eventually they might purchase their freedom.[42]

The Role of Women

Athenian women, wealthy and poor alike, also contributed to the city's prosperity by assuming many essential duties, such as child rearing, housekeeping, and making clothes. Susan Peach explained that each day, an Athenian wife

> inspected the stores [household supplies], and ensured that the house was clean and tidy and that meals were ready on time. She looked after the children and any sick members of the household, and managed the family finances. The women of the household produced all the cloth needed for clothes and furnishings. Spinning and weaving therefore occupied a large amount of a wife's time.[43]

By modern standards, Athenian women lived sheltered, restricted lives. They could not take part in government and were expected to obey their fathers and husbands. Women also stayed at home most of the time, usually going out only for religious festivals, to attend the theater, or to do personal shopping. When in public, they had to be accompanied by a slave or other attendant. Describing what was expected of women, the Greek historian Xenophon wrote:

> You will need to stay indoors. . . . Over those whose appointed tasks are indoors it will be your duty to preside. . . . The greatest joy of all will be to prove yourself . . . a better helpmate to myself and to the children, a better guardian of our home, so will your honor increase. . . . [By being dutiful] you will enjoy your food, grow vigorous in health, and your complexion will in very truth be lovelier.[44]

In general, Athenian men agreed with Pericles, who said that women should keep out of men's affairs and be "spoken of as little as possible, whether for good or ill."[45]

Yet this view of women's worth was often more official than actual. Despite their second-class citizenship, women played a more important role in Athenian life than the men liked to admit. By performing their important daily tasks, women freed their husbands to take part in government, serve in the military, and pursue cultural endeavors. A few Athenian women even acquired the same respect as men. For example, Pericles contradicted his official view of women and openly praised Aspasia, his second wife. According to Plutarch, "Pericles made his court to [courted] Aspasia only on account of her wisdom and political abilities. Even Socrates [the great philosopher] himself sometimes visited her along with his friends. . . . Pericles took Aspasia [as his wife], for whom he had the tenderest regard, for he never went out upon business or returned without [expressing his love for her]."[46]

Greek women typically spent most of their time engaged in household activities. Many found embroidery, shown here, to be pleasurable as well as useful.

This scene from a Greek vase shows students learning poetry and music. The standing figures are the teachers, called kitharistes.

The Pursuit of Knowledge

Because few women took part in government or produced art and literature, they received no formal education. Both poor and wealthy young men, on the other hand, received extensive schooling. This was to prepare them for politics, for military service and leadership, and for enriching the city's cultural life as artists, craftsmen, athletes, musicians, and poets. Between the ages of seven and eighteen, all boys attended three kinds of schools. In the first, teachers called *grammatistes* taught them reading, writing, and mathematics. In another school, boys learned music and poetry from instructors known as *kitharistes.* Finally, boys went to a training ground called a gymnasium, where they learned dancing and athletics, including wrestling and throwing the discus. At age eighteen, all young men received military training, after which they stood before the city council and recited the following oath:

I will not disgrace the sacred arms, nor will I abandon the man next to me [in battle], whoever he may be. I will bring

aid to the ritual of the state. . . . I will obey those who from time to time are judges; I will obey the established statutes [laws] and whatever other regulations the people shall enact. If anyone shall attempt to destroy the statutes, I will not permit it, but will repel him. . . . I will honor the ancestral faith.[47]

Higher education took several forms. Some young men studied as apprentices under great sculptors, artists, or architects. Others learned public speaking, astronomy, geometry, geography, and other subjects from traveling teachers called sophists, who charged a fee for their services. Other teachers, called philosophers, did not charge a fee. The philosophers held informal meetings in the marketplace or in a gymnasium. They challenged their young listeners to consider questions about morality, the definitions of good and evil, and what constituted happiness and a good life.

The most famous Athenian philosopher was Socrates, who began teaching toward the end of the golden age. He produced no writings of his own. What is known about his life and ideas comes from the writings of his pupils—the historian Xenophon and the philosopher Plato, who taught in the fourth century B.C. According to Xenophon, Socrates was "so just that he wronged no man in the most trifling affair . . . so wise that he never erred in distinguishing better from worse . . . so capable of discerning the character of others, and of [teaching] them virtue and honor, that he seemed to be such as the best and happiest of men would be." Plato called Socrates "truly the wisest, and justest, and best of all the men whom I have ever known."[48]

Socrates proposed that goodness stems from knowledge about one's self and the world, while evil and wickedness are the result of ignorance. He believed that the search for truth and self-knowledge is the noblest of human endeavors. According to Plato, Socrates once told an Athenian: "My good sir, you are an Athenian, a citizen of the city which is greatest and most noted for its wisdom and power; are you not then ashamed to be worrying about your money and how to increase it, and about your reputation, and about your honor, instead of worrying about the knowledge of good and truth and how to improve your soul?"[49]

Rather than lecturing, Socrates taught by asking his pupils questions and pretending to be ignorant of the answers. This encouraged them to discover the truth of a situation on their own in a step-by-step process. This process later became known as the Socratic method in his honor. Socrates taught many Athenians to take pride in themselves and in their city, saying that both were potential sources of wisdom.

The Culmination of Culture

Athenians also took pride in their city because of its beauty. In 449, Pericles proposed that the Athenians rebuild the temples on the Acropolis that had been

This nineteenth-century European painting depicts the philosopher Socrates instructing the brilliant but unprincipled Alcibiades, who would later betray his country.

A modern reconstruction of a classical Greek temple. Such structures were decorated in reds, blues, and other bright colors.

destroyed by the Persians. This would not only improve and beautify the city, he said, but also put thousands of people to work. Plutarch reported:

> That which gave most pleasure and ornament to the city of Athens, and the greatest admiration and even astonishment to all strangers . . . was his [Pericles'] construction of the public and sacred buildings. . . . It being his desire and design that . . . these vast projects of buildings and designs of works . . . would give employment to numerous arts, so that [a majority of the people might receive] the benefit and have their share of the public moneys. The materials were stone, brass, ivory, gold, ebony cypress-wood; and the arts or trades that wrought and fashioned them were smiths and carpenters, molders [trim carvers], founders [metal casters] and braziers [brass workers], stone-cutters, dyers, goldsmiths . . . painters . . . merchants and mariners and ship-masters by sea, and by land, cartwrights [cart makers]cattle-breeders, waggoners, rope-makers . . . road-makers, miners.[50]

The new Parthenon, temple of the goddess Athena, was the largest and most magnificent building on the Acropolis. Designed by the architect Ictinus and the sculptor Phidias and completed in 438 B.C., the building was 237 feet long, 110 feet wide, and 60 feet high. It required some twenty-two thousand tons of marble. Inside stood Phidias's dazzling, forty-foot-high statue of the goddess. This sculpture of wood, ivory, and more than twenty-five hundred pounds of pure gold cost nearly five million drachmas, a huge sum at the time. So impressive was the Parthenon that a later traveler to Athens was moved to remark, "All the world's culture culminated in Greece, all Greece in Athens, all Athens in its Acropolis, all the Acropolis in the Parthenon."[51] The Parthenon and other buildings on the Acropolis became the focal point of Athenian worship, religious festivals, and city-wide celebrations. These structures also became symbols of Athens's prosperity and its people's talent and love of beauty.

Tragedy and Comedy

The theater was another example of Athenian talent and cultural awareness. Crowds of people regularly flocked to the city's theaters, including the largest, the Theater of Dionysus, nestled on one side of the Acropolis. In this open-air structure that seated at least seventeen thousand, audiences watched plays depicting a wide range of subjects. Some were about the gods and the Age of Heroes. Others dramatized more recent events, such as the Persian Wars. The presentations were colorful, employing elaborate scenery, costumes, and music, and the actors wore masks so that spectators in the rear seats could better distinguish the characters. Athenian audiences were almost as colorful as the plays they watched. "Men and women of all ranks are admitted," explained Will Durant.

> Women sit apart from men, and courtesans [prostitutes] have a place to themselves. . . . It is a lively audience. . . . It eats nuts and fruit and drinks wine as it listens. . . . It quarrels about seats, claps and shouts for its favorites, hisses and groans when it is displeased; when moved to more vigorous protest it kicks the benches beneath it; if it becomes angry it may frighten an actor off the stage with olives, figs, or stones.[52]

The four most important Athenian playwrights were Aeschylus, Sophocles, Euripides, and Aristophanes. The first three produced mostly tragedies, serious dramas

Among the sculptures adorning Athens's Theater of Dionysus, right, is the "Crouching Silenus," left. The sileni were fertility spirits associated with the god Dionysus.

Splendor of the Parthenon

The magnificent buildings adorning the Acropolis in Athens, constructed to replace those destroyed by the Persians in 480 B.C., are among the most beautiful and famous ever built. Here, historian James Henry Breasted provides a glimpse of the great sculptor Phidias at work and a portrait of the Acropolis in its original, majestic state:

"Now at last Pericles has undertaken the restoration of the ancient shrines on a scale of magnificence and beauty before unknown anywhere in the Greek world. . . . As he looks up at the gleaming marble shafts he feels that the architectural splendor now crowning the Acropolis is the work of the Athenian *people*. . . . From the height above, the tinkle of many distant hammers tells where the stonecutters are shaping the marble blocks for the still unfinished Parthenon, a noble temple dedicated to Athena; and there, too, the people often see Pericles intently inspecting the building, as Phidias the sculptor and Ictinus the architect of the building pace up and down the inclosure, explaining to him the progress of the work. It was in these wondrous Greek buildings that the architect and sculptor working hand in hand produced a marvelously harmonious result. . . . In a long band of carved marble extending entirely around the four sides of the Parthenon . . . Phidias and his pupils have portrayed, as in a glorified vision, the sovereign [free] people of Athens moving in [a] stately procession. . . . Inside the new temple gleams the colossal figure of Athena, wrought by the cunning hand of Phidias in gold and ivory. Even from the city below the citizen can discern, touched with bright colors, the heroic figures of the gods with which Phidias has filled the triangular gable ends of the building. Out in the open area behind the colonnaded entrance rises another great work of Phidias, a colossal bronze statue of Athena, seventy feet high as it stands on its tall base. With shield and spear the goddess stands, the gracious protectress of Athens, and the glittering point of her gilded [golden] spear can be seen shining like a beacon far across the land, even by the sailors as they round the promontory of Mount Hymettus and sail homeward."

about love and hate, war, betrayal, and the wrath of the gods. The speeches, set in poetic verse, were often moving, as in the following lines from Sophocles' *Antigone*. A king who has ordered a young girl to be buried alive finds that she has hanged herself and that her lover, his own son, plans to follow her in death:

> We looked, and in the cavern's vaulted
>   gloom
> I saw the maiden lying strangled there,
> A noose of linen twined about her
>   neck;
> And hard beside her, clasping her cold
>   form,
> Her lover lay bewailing his dead
>   bride . . .
> When the King saw him, with a terrible groan
> He moved towards him, crying, "O my
>   son,
> What hast thou done? What ailed
>   thee?" . . .
> But the son glared at him with tiger
>   eyes,
> Spat in his face, and then, without a
>   word . . .
> Fell on his sword and drove it through
>   his side
> Home; but, yet breathing, clasped in
>   his lax arms
> The maid, her pallid [pale] cheek
>   [bloodied]
> With his expiring [dying] gasps. So
>   there they lay
> Two corpses, one in death.[53]

By contrast, the comic plays of Aristophanes were lighthearted and filled with slapstick, often vulgar humor. Aristophanes and other comedy writers wrote mostly satires, fictional stories that poked fun at real customs, institutions, politi-

Comedic playwright Aristophanes. Of his forty-three plays, eleven have survived.

cians, military leaders, and even respected philosophers. For instance, in *Clouds*, Aristophanes depicts a country gentleman named Strepsiades visiting Socrates and his pupils at the "Think-shop." Seeing most of the pupils bent over with their noses on the ground, Strepsiades approaches another student:

> STREPSIADES   What manner of beasts
>   are these?. . . Why are their eyes
>   riveted to the ground?
> STUDENT   They are investigating
>   what's under it. . . .
> STREPSIADES   Then why does [that
>   fellow's] rump gaze heavenward?
> STUDENT   His secondary interest is
>   astronomy.[54]

An Education for Greece

Athenian cultural endeavors also included scientific theory and experimentation. One of the most important Greek scientists was Anaxagoras, who migrated from Ionia to Athens during the golden age. He was one of several original thinkers of the day who challenged traditional views of nature and the universe, such as the belief that the heavenly bodies were controlled by the gods. The sun was not the brightness surrounding the god Helios, declared Anaxagoras. "The sun is a red-hot mass many times larger than the Peloponnesus," he said. He was also the first to recognize that the moon does not give off its own light but shines by reflected light. Anaxagoras also correctly explained how eclipses work. "The moon is eclipsed through the interposition of the earth [between sun and moon] . . . the sun through the interposition of the moon [between sun and earth]."[55] These theories were readily accepted by many Greeks at the time.

Other Greek scientists also tried to explain the wonders of nature in a logical manner. Leucippus and Democritus, both Ionians who frequently worked in Athens, proposed that all matter is composed of tiny particles that cannot be broken down into smaller particles. Democritus called these particles atoms. Later, modern scientists proved this idea to be correct. And a doctor named Hippocrates, who often practiced in Athens, suggested that illness was not the work of gods and demons. Diseases had natural causes, he said, and therefore people could cure them. Hippocrates' greatest contribution was the Hippocratic oath, a doctor's pledge to heal the sick at all costs, to which modern doctors still swear.

In a few short years, Athens underwent an unprecedented cultural explosion, and Pericles achieved his goal of creating a model city. "I say that the whole city is an education for Greece," he declared. "This is no passing boast in speech, but truth and fact. . . . For when put to the test, Athens alone among her contemporaries is superior."[56] New freedoms, new knowledge, and enlightened leaders had together produced a fresh new view of the human condition. This view stressed the importance of the individual, of the creative spirit, and of the search for truth using logic and reason.

But what historian Edith Hamilton called Athens's "brief and magnificent flowering of genius"[57] was not enough to assure the city's dominance in Greece. While the Athenians erected their temples and attended their theaters, their empire began to fall apart. One by one, Athens's subject poleis in the Delian League rebelled. And Sparta and its neighbors, ever jealous of Athenian success, plotted the fall of Pericles' proud city. This time, when the war trumpets sounded, no foreign enemy would be waiting on the battlefield. It would be Greek against Greek.

Hippocrates, whose oath became the sacred pledge of all doctors.

Chapter

6 Greek Versus Greek: The Peloponnesian War

It was, perhaps, inevitable that the two great Greek powers—Athens and Sparta—would eventually fight each other. Each was convinced that it alone should enjoy supremacy in Greece. And after decades of tensions, mistrust, and rivalry between these cities, each finally reached a point where it was willing to fight a major war to gain that supremacy.

But though their differences caused the war, the fighting involved and affected more than just the Athenians and Spartans. Each city drew its allies into the conflict, which widened to engulf the whole Greek world. Thucydides, in his history of the war, reported that Athens and Sparta "were then at the full height of their military power." He wrote that he "saw the rest of the Greeks either siding or intending to side with one or the other. No other movement [event] ever stirred Greece more deeply than this."[58] Indeed, for the Greeks it was an ordeal of total war that proved ruinous for all involved. The bloody conflict lasted twenty-seven grueling years, caused widespread death and misery, and exhausted the resources and energies of all involved. The war also caused the downfall of Athens and the end of its glorious golden age.

The Spartans and Syracusans annihilate the Athenian army in Sicily in 413 B.C., the worst military disaster in Athens's history.

The Causes of the War

One major underlying cause of the war was Sparta's deep mistrust of Athens. Trying to check Athenian expansion, Sparta had backed many of the rebellions against Athens by members of the Delian League in the 440s and 430s. But these efforts had only momentarily weakened the wealthy and powerful Athenians. Sparta longed to defeat its rival, disband the Athenian empire, and eliminate democracy. The Spartans, however, still slow to take action, kept putting off declaring an all-out war on Athens.

Athens was also to blame for the war because it had created an atmosphere of hostility among both its opponents and allies. Though it had established the Delian League with good intentions, Athens had eventually resorted to force to keep it and the Athenian empire intact. Many Greeks, even some Athenians, regularly objected to Athens's use of money from the league treasury. Believing the Athenians to be unfair and tyrannical, a number of Athens's former allies eagerly joined the growing anti-Athenian alliance led by Sparta.

The immediate cause of the war was a series of events involving one of Sparta's allies—Corinth. This polis, located in the northeastern Peloponnesus, had its own reasons for hating Athens. In 435, a civil war erupted between democrats and oligarchs on the island of Corcyra, a Corinthian colony located off the northwestern coast of Greece. The oligarchs asked Corinth, itself an oligarchy, for help. But when the mother polis sent warships, the Corcyrean democrats defeated them. When Corinth prepared to send a larger force, the democrats appealed to Athens for aid. In 433, a combined force of Cor-

This map of the Peloponnesus shows Sparta and some of its allies in its war with Athens.

cyrean and Athenian warships gave Corinth a second naval defeat. The enraged Corinthians turned to Sparta, asking that it mobilize its army and rid Greece of the impudent Athenians once and for all. The Corinthian envoys told the Spartans:

> Time after time we have warned you of the mischief which the Athenians would do to us. . . . They are at this moment intriguing [plotting] against others, notably against allies of ours. . . . In the face of such an enemy, Spartans, you persist in doing nothing. But let your procrastination [putting things off] end. Do not allow friends and kindred to fall into the hands of their worst enemies. . . . You have inherited from your fathers the leadership of Peloponnesus; see that her greatness suffers no diminution [loss] at your hands.[59]

The Athenians were aware of what Corinth was doing and feared that a major war was imminent. Pericles convinced other

Athenian leaders that the way to avert war was to put on a display of Athenian power. Such a show of force, he argued, might make Sparta and its allies think twice about fighting Athens. So the Athenians imposed a trade embargo against one of Sparta's most important allies—Megara, located on the Isthmus of Corinth, about halfway between Athens and Corinth. This prohibited the Megarians from dealing at any port controlled by Athens. Because Athens controlled so many Mediterranean ports, Megara could not import enough food to sustain itself and the Megarians began to starve. Viewing this as the final Athenian insult, Sparta declared war on Athens in 431.

The Combatants Draw Their Plans

The conflict, the most destructive in Greek history, came to be known as the Peloponnesian War because Athens's primary opponents—Sparta and Corinth—resided in the Peloponnesus. Sparta's other allies included Megara, Thebes, and Phocis, all lying directly west or north of Athens. Sparta's goal was to attack Attica by land, burn its houses, and lay waste to the countryside. This, the Spartans hoped, would disrupt agriculture and spread fear and chaos through the region, eventually persuading the Athenians to surrender. Sparta and its allies, therefore, quickly assembled a formidable army of about thirty thousand hoplites in the Isthmus of Corinth.

Athens's allies included Corcyra, most of the Aegean islands and Ionian cities, and all of Athens's colonies. Especially important to Athens were its colonies along the coasts of the Black Sea, which provided the city with essential supplies of grain and other food. Without these supplies, Athens could not feed its large population. Realizing that trying to defeat the Spartan army would be foolhardy, the Athenians adopted a plan that relied on their fleet. Pericles ordered the entire population of Attica to take refuge behind the Long Walls. Athenian cargo ships would then support them while the city's warships disrupted enemy trade and attacked towns on the coasts of the Peloponnesus. Eventually, Pericles hoped, the Spartans would grow tired and frustrated and give up the fight.

At first, the Athenian plan seemed to work. In the summer of 431, the Spartans, led by their king, Archidamus, marched

Pericles declared, "I am more afraid of our mistakes than the enemy's plans."

Pericles delivering his famous funeral oration, in which he predicted that Athens's glory would live forever.

During that first winter, most of the people of Athens gathered to mourn the few Athenians who had died in the initial fighting. Pericles delivered a funeral oration that is now regarded as one of the greatest speeches in history. He praised Athens, saying that its democratic values were well worth dying for. Then, he said of the fallen soldiers:

> It seems to me that a death such as theirs . . . gives the true measure of a man's worth. . . . In the face of death they resolved to rely upon themselves alone. And when the moment came they [decided] to resist and suffer, rather than to fly and save their lives. . . . On the battlefield their feet stood fast, and in an instant, at the height of their fortune, they passed away from the scene [died], not of their fear, but of their glory. Such was the end of these men; they were worthy of Athens. . . . I would have you day by day fix your eyes upon the greatness of Athens, until you become filled with the love of her; and when you are impressed with the spectacle of her glory, reflect that this empire has been acquired by men who knew their duty and had the courage to do it.[61]

Disease and Battle Take Their Toll

into Attica and burned Athenian homes and farms. But this accomplished little because Athens maintained nearly complete control of the seas. As Pericles promised, Athenian ships kept the inhabitants of the city well supplied while they also successfully raided enemy coasts. "The Athenian forces," Thucydides recalled, "which had lately been dispatched to [the] Peloponnesus in the hundred vessels, and were assisted by the Corcyreans with fifty ships . . . did considerable damage on the Peloponnesian coast."[60] When winter came, the Spartans and their allies returned to the warmth of their homes in the Peloponnesus. This left the Athenians free to leave the Long Walls and rebuild some of their own homes.

In the spring of 430, the Spartans invaded Attica once more. The Athenians, confident in the plan that had been so successful the year before, retreated again behind the Long Walls. This time, however, they had to deal with an unexpected enemy, for a terrible plague struck the city, spreading with frightening swiftness through the crowded streets. The Athenians were unfamiliar with the disease, which remains unidentified. According to Thucydides' gripping eyewitness account:

> People in good health were all of a sudden attacked by violent heats in the head and redness and inflammation in the eyes, the inward parts such as the throat or tongue becoming bloody and emitting an unnatural and fetid [disgusting] breath. . . . In most cases also . . . retching [vomiting] followed, producing violent spasms. . . . Even where it did not prove mortal [fatal], it still left its mark on the extremities; for it settled in the . . . fingers and the toes, and many escaped with the loss of these, some too with that of their eyes.[62]

In only a few months, about 20 percent of Athens's population perished from the disease. To make matters worse, before the plague ran its course, it struck down Pericles himself, who died in 429.

With Pericles gone, two factions fought for power in Athens. One, led by a politician named Cleon, wanted to keep fighting until Athens had gained a clear victory. The other, more conservative faction, led by a wealthy citizen named Nicias, favored making peace. For several years, the Assembly backed Cleon's more aggressive policies and the war continued.

As the years went on, the conflict claimed many lives and caused much destruction on both sides. Each spring, the Athenians hid inside the Long Walls while the Spartans burned and pillaged the countryside of Attica. At the same time, Athenian warships kept up their raids on enemy shipping and coastal towns. Period-

ically, one side enjoyed a stunning victory. In 427, for instance, the Spartans besieged and destroyed Athens's longtime ally Plataea, killing or enslaving the inhabitants. Athens countered in 425 by capturing and occupying the Spartan coastal town of Pilos. More bloody fighting followed until 422, when both Cleon and Brasidas, Sparta's ablest general, died in battle. Nicias now won over the Athenian assembly. He made peace overtures to Sparta and in 421, both sides, weary of war, agreed to a treaty known as the Peace of Nicias.

Disaster at Syracuse

But the treaty never actually went into effect. This was partly because Sparta's allies, especially Corinth and Thebes, refused to

The traitor Alcibiades, whose military advice to Sparta helped defeat Athens.

A Good-Looking and Talented Scoundrel

The Athenian traitor Alcibiades was one of the most colorful leaders in history. He was a man who believed in doing whatever was necessary to get ahead in life, even if it was unpopular or morally wrong. In his Lives, *Plutarch offered insights into Alcibiades' headstrong character in the following anecdotes. The first two incidents are from his childhood, and the third concerns his treatment of his wife, Hipparete:*

"Alcibiades' manners were far from being uniform. . . . He was naturally a man of strong passions, but the ruling one was an ambition to contend [argue] and overcome. This appears from anecdotes told of him as a boy. When hard pressed in wrestling, to prevent his being thrown, he bit the hands of his antagonist [opponent], who let go his hold and said: 'You bite, Alcibiades, like a woman.' 'No,' he replied, 'like a lion.'

One day he was playing at dice with other boys in the street and when it came to his turn . . . a loaded wagon came up. At first he called to the driver to stop because he was to throw in the way over which the wagon was to pass. The [driver] disregarded him and drove on, the other boys broke away, but Alcibiades threw himself upon his face directly before the wagon and, stretching himself out, bade the fellow to drive on if he pleased. Upon this the man was so startled that he stopped his horses. . . .

Hipparete made a prudent and affectionate wife, but at last, growing very uneasy at her husband's associating with such a number of courtesans [prostitutes], both strangers and Athenians, she left his house and went to her brother's. Alcibiades pursued his debaucheries [lusts] and was not concerned with his wife, but it was necessary for her, in order to obtain a legal separation, to give in a bill of divorce to the archon and to appear personally with it, for the sending of it by another hand would not do. When she came to do this according to law, Alcibiades rushed in, caught her in his arms and carried her through the marketplace to his own house, no one presuming [daring] to oppose him or take her from him. From that time on she remained with him [against her will] until her death."

acknowledge it. They wanted no peace until Athens was destroyed. Also, a new war leader came to power in Athens—Alcibiades—a larger-than-life character who won the hearts of the people. According to Plutarch, the Athenians loved him for "his great abilities in politics . . . the reach of his genius . . . the beauty of his person, the force of his eloquence [speaking skills], together with his heroic strength, his valor and experience in war."[63] But Alcibiades was also conceited, unprincipled, and preoccupied with enhancing his own reputation as a war hero. Hoping to revive the war against a weakened Sparta, he persuaded some of Sparta's Peloponnesian allies to rebel against Sparta. This provoked the Spartans into resuming the conflict with Athens, just as Alcibiades had wanted. But Sparta's still-mighty army easily defeated the rebels, and Athens once more faced the full strength of the Spartan alliance.

In 415, Alcibiades suggested a daring, and what seemed to some Athenians foolhardy, scheme. He proposed that Athens send a powerful naval expedition to Sicily, south of Italy, and conquer Syracuse, the strongest and most influential of the island's many Greek cities. Defeating Syracuse, Alcibiades argued, would give Athens control of all Sicily. With the wealth, foodstuffs, and soldiers of Sicily at its disposal, Athens could then easily defeat Sparta and its allies. Despite the misgivings of some Athenians, Alcibiades managed to convince the Assembly to back the expedition. Although Nicias was against the venture, the Athenians gave him shared command with Alcibiades in hopes of fostering political unity. According to Plutarch, the mighty fleet had "near a hundred and forty galleys . . . five thousand one hundred heavy-armed soldiers and about a

thousand three hundred archers, slingers and others . . . with suitable provisions."[64]

Although most Athenians believed this formidable force would be successful, the expedition to Syracuse quickly turned into the greatest single disaster in Athens's history. Shortly after the fleet sailed, some of Alcibiades' enemies in Athens accused him of earlier defacing some religious statues. When the government sent a messenger to recall him for trial, he fled and turned traitor by seeking refuge in Sparta. This left Nicias, an incompetent commander, in charge of the expedition. Arriving at Syracuse, he blockaded the city's harbor, but he was slow in mounting a full-scale attack.

While Nicias delayed, Alcibiades convinced the Spartans that they could deal Athens a death blow by sending troops to help the Syracusans. When the Spartan forces arrived, Nicias immediately appealed to Athens for reinforcements. Nicias wrote, "The time . . . has come for you to decide either to recall us, or else to send out another force, both naval and

Athenian warships threaten Syracuse. Each ship, rowed by over one hundred slaves, carried from forty to fifty soldiers.

The Spartans inflict heavy casualties as they pursue the retreating Athenians across the Sicilian countryside near Syracuse.

military, as big as the first, with large sums of money."[65] The reinforcements arrived, but further Athenian delays allowed the Syracusans and Spartans to trap the fleets along the Sicilian coast. In the autumn of 413, the Athenians suffered a humiliating defeat, losing most of their ships. The survivors then fled to shore and tried desperately to organize some kind of defense. Thucydides recalled that they

> were in a dreadful condition. . . . They had lost their whole fleet. . . . The dead were unburied. . . . There was also a general feeling of shame. . . . They had come intending to enslave others, and they were going away in fear that they would be themselves enslaved. . . . [Soon] the Syracusans and

the allies . . . assailed them on every side, hurling javelins and other missiles at them. The Athenians hurried on to the river Assinarus. They hoped to gain a little relief if they forded the river, for . . . they were worn out by fatigue and thirst. But no sooner did they reach the water than they lost all order and rushed in. . . . They fell upon one another, and trampled each other under foot: some at once perished, pierced by their own spears. . . . The Syracusans stood upon the further bank of the river . . . and hurled missiles from above on the Athenians. . . . The Spartans came down the bank and slaughtered them . . . the water at once became foul [with blood]. . . . At last, when the dead bodies were lying in heaps upon one another in the water . . . Nicias surrendered.[66]

After the defeat, the Syracusans executed Nicias and the other Athenian commanders. All of the other Athenian survivors became slaves in Sicilian stone quarries and eventually died of exhaustion, starvation, and mistreatment.

The Fall of Athens

Despite these grim losses, Athens refused to surrender. It built new fleets and tried to carry on the war. But the advantage in the conflict steadily shifted toward Sparta. The Athenians found themselves running out of money while their allies abandoned them. Also, the Spartans, on the advice of Alcibiades, set up permanent forts in Attica, forcing the Athenians to remain behind the Long Walls year-round. The

The Streets Piled with Corpses

Much of what is known about the disastrous war between Athens and Sparta comes from Thucydides' brilliant eyewitness account The Peloponnesian Wars. *The following excerpt is his vivid, horrifying description of the plague that struck Athens at the height of the war:*

"The other victims who were in perfect health, all in a moment . . . were seized first with violent heats in the head and with redness and burning of the eyes. Internally, the throat and the tongue at once became blood-red, and the breath abnormal and fetid [foul]. Sneezing and hoarseness followed; in a short time the disorder, accompanied by a violent cough, reached the chest. . . . An ineffectual retching [vomiting], producing violent convulsions, attacked most of the sufferers. . . . The body externally was not so very hot to the touch, not yellowish but flushed . . . and breaking out in blisters and ulcers [sores]. But the internal fever was intense; the sufferers could not bear to have on them even the lightest linen garment; they insisted on being naked, and there was nothing which they longed for more eagerly than to throw themselves into cold water. . . . They were tormented by unceasing thirst. . . . They could find no way of resting, and sleeplessness attacked them throughout. . . . Thus, most died on the seventh or ninth day of internal fever. . . . At the same time diarrhea set in which was uniformly fluid. . . . The character of the malady no words can describe, and the fury with which it fastened upon each sufferer was too much for human nature to endure. There was one circumstance in particular which distinguished it from ordinary diseases. Although so many bodies were lying unburied, the birds and animals which feed on human flesh either never came near them or died if they touched them. . . . Equally appalling was the fact that men died like sheep, catching the infection if they attended on one another; and this was the principal cause of mortality [death]. . . . The crowding of the people out of the country into the city aggravated the misery. . . . The dead and the dying lay one upon another, while others hardly alive rolled in the streets and around every fountain craving water. The temples in which they lodged were full of the corpses of those who died in them."

As musicians play, the Spartans force the Athenians to tear down the Long Walls after Athens's surrender in 404 B.C. Athens had to forfeit most of its ships and all of its foreign possessions.

residents of Athens grew increasingly weary of living in crowded, unsanitary conditions.

In addition, the Spartans now realized that the key to defeating Athens was naval power. Sparta had no war fleets of its own and lacked the money to build them, so in 412, it made an alliance with its former enemy Persia. The Persians were only too glad to supply money to ensure Athens's destruction, and the Spartans built their fleet. For several years, Athens held its own against this new Spartan threat. As long as the grain route to the Black Sea colonies remained open and Athens could feed itself, the city's leaders reasoned, a chance for victory remained. But the Spartans finally cut that vital lifeline. In 405, the Spartan navy inflicted a major defeat on the Athenians at Aegospotami, on the coast of Thrace. This gave the Spartans control of the northern Aegean and the grain route.

When the Athenians received word of this catastrophe, Xenophon wrote that

> a bitter wail of woe broke forth. From Piraeus, following the line of the Long Walls up to the heart of the city, it swept and swelled, as each man and his neighbor passed on the news. On that night no man slept. There was mourning and sorrow for those that were lost, but the lamentation [grief] was merged in even greater sorrow for themselves, as they pictured the evils they were about to suffer.[67]

Exhausted, their wealth depleted, and their supply line severed, the Athenians surrendered in 404. The victorious Spartans tore down the Long Walls, abolished Athenian democracy, and replaced it with an oligarchy. Athens's brief but glorious age of empire and cultural greatness was over.

Chapter

7 Alexander's Conquests: The Spread of Greek Culture

Following the Peloponnesian War, Greece entered a period of decline. The war had killed tens of thousands of people, devastated hundreds of towns and cities, and left the city-states more disunited than ever. At first, because of its victory over Athens, Sparta dominated Greek affairs. But the Spartans failed to maintain this dominance, partly because they were not able administrators. Also, they tried to force many poleis to conform to Sparta's conservative ideas and political system. During the first three decades of the fourth century B.C., Spartan misrule and bully tactics provoked a series of small but damaging wars between Sparta and various other city-states. These largely indecisive conflicts further exhausted the already war-weary Greek cities. Finally, in 371, in the battle of Leuctra, Thebes delivered the once invincible Spartan army a crushing defeat, forever eliminating Sparta as a major Greek power. But neither Thebes nor Athens, which had restored its democracy during these years, nor any other polis had enough strength left to claim supremacy in Greece.

Weak and vulnerable to outside attack, the Greeks were ill prepared for the emergence of a great military power in their own backyard. In the middle of the fourth century B.C., the scattered, warlike tribes

of Macedonia, in extreme northern Greece, united. The Greeks had always looked upon the Macedonians as semicivilized and incapable barbarians. So they largely ignored Macedonia as it amassed a formidable military force. This was a grave mistake. Under their effective war leader, King Philip II, the Macedonians would prove themselves both civilized and capable. They would succeed, where the other city-states had failed, at uniting the country. And Philip's brilliant son, Alexander the Great, would, by conquest, spread Greek culture and ideas across most of the known world.

King Philip II, whose development of the devastating Macedonian phalanx helped him conquer Greece.

A Quest for Power and Culture

The rise of Macedonia as a great power began when Philip ascended to the throne in 359. At the time, many Macedonians belonged to backward and fiercely independent hill tribes that had given allegiance to the previous kings only when it was convenient. As a result, the country was disorganized and weak. Philip, desiring to make Macedonia strong, set about subduing and unifying the tribes. He was successful, partly because he was a power-hungry and ruthless leader and also because of his shrewdness and talent as a general. In only three years, Philip unified most of the country and amassed and trained a powerful army.

Part of what made the Macedonian army effective was Philip's introduction of an important military innovation. For centuries, the Greeks had sometimes used a battle formation called a phalanx, in which soldiers stood in several lines, or ranks, one directly behind another. The forward motion of the rear ranks gave extra strength and momentum to the front lines. Philip gave the troops in the rear ranks of the phalanx longer and longer spears, so that a mass of spears projected from the front,

The Macedonian phalanx in action. The formation eventually became sixteen ranks deep, the spears ranging in length from nine to twenty-one feet.

Aristotle lectures Alexander in the Temple of the Nymphs near the Macedonian town of Mieza.

giving the formation the look of a huge porcupine. Neither regular foot soldiers nor the cavalry had a chance of penetrating the Macedonian phalanx.

After unifying Macedonia, Philip gazed with envious eyes on Athens and the other splendid cultural centers of southern Greece. He planned to take advantage of the weakness and disunity of the Greek poleis and make himself master of all Greece. He also wanted to acquire the refinements of Greek culture for himself and for his people and dreamed of making his capital of Pella, in southern Macedonia, a new center of Greek learning.

Philip began this culturization process with his own son, Alexander, born in 356.

Are Foreigners Slaves by Nature?

Alexander's attitude toward the Persians and other foreign peoples was profoundly influenced by his tutor Aristotle. Aristotle maintained rigidly conservative and traditional views on some subjects. For instance, according to Peter Green in his book Alexander the Great, *Aristotle believed that non-Greeks were slaves by nature:*

"It was therefore right and fitting for Greeks to rule over barbarians [non-Greeks], but not for barbarians to rule over Greeks. Like most intellectuals with a racialist [racist] ax to grind, Aristotle drew facts from geopolitics or 'natural law' in support of his thesis. In a celebrated fragment he counselled Alexander 'to be a *hegemon* [leader] to the Greeks and a despot to the barbarians, to look after the former as after friends and relatives, and to deal with the latter as with beasts or plants.' In this, he had the whole body of Greek civilized opinion behind him; and there is no reason to suppose that Alexander, to begin with, did not wholeheartedly share his racialist views. Barbarians, it is clear, were to be despised above all *because they lived exclusively through and for the senses* [for pleasure]. This doctrine must have had a strong appeal for Alexander, who always placed a premium on self-control and self-denial."

The boy had the finest Greek tutors his father's money could buy, and he proved to be an excellent student. "He had," wrote Plutarch, "a violent thirst and passion for learning, which increased as time went on. . . . He was a lover of all kinds of reading and knowledge."[68] Eventually, Philip asked the renowned Athenian philosopher, Aristotle, to teach Alexander. Aristotle tutored the boy in ethics, politics, science, and other subjects and taught him that the main goal of human life is to find happiness. A happy life, said Aristotle, is one governed by logic and reason. The philosopher strongly believed that the Greeks were morally and culturally superior to all other peoples and instilled this idea in Alexander. Aristotle also helped shape the boy's ideas about war, saying that war was justified under certain conditions. First, men could wage war "in order that . . . they may themselves avoid becoming enslaved to others; [second] so that they may seek control for the benefit of the subject people . . . and thirdly to hold despotic [total] power over those who deserve to be slaves."[69] Alexander would later use these ideas to justify his conquest and rule of foreign peoples.

Master of the Greeks

While Alexander was growing up, Philip began his conquest of Greece. First, the king marched his army southward into Thessaly, taking complete control of the territory by 353. In the following year, Philip attacked and conquered Thrace, to the east of Macedonia. He now controlled most of the Greek lands north of the pass

The orator Demosthenes. Plutarch wrote of his "passion for distinction and love of liberty."

of Thermopylae. While most Athenians and other Greeks continued casually to ignore these aggressions, a few were worried enough to shout warnings. Among them was Demosthenes, an influential Athenian orator. Beginning in 351, he delivered a series of compelling speeches, which became known as the philippics because they dealt with Philip. Demosthenes called Philip a threatening barbarian and urged Athenians and other Greeks to rise up and stop the Macedonians before it was too late. "Observe, Athenians," said Demosthenes,

the height to which the fellow's insolence has soared: he leaves you no choice of action or inaction; he blusters and talks big. . . . He cannot rest content with what he has conquered; he is always taking in more, everywhere casting his net round us, while we sit idle and do nothing. When, Athenians, will you take the necessary action? What are you waiting for? Until you are compelled, I presume. But what are we to think of what is happening now? For my own part I think that for a free people there can be no greater compulsion than shame for their [present passive] position.[70]

For a few years, most Athenians and other Greeks did not heed Demosthenes' warnings. But when Philip moved into southern Greece and took control of the shrines at Delphi in 346, many Greeks began to flock to the orator's cause. Eventually, Demosthenes convinced longtime enemies Athens and Thebes to unite in an attempt to repel the Macedonians.

On August 4, 338, the united Greek army of thirty-five thousand hoplites met Philip's forces, numbering about thirty thousand, at Chaeronea, to the west of Thebes. Leading the Theban contingent was the Sacred Band, a group of elite troops that had defeated the Spartans at Leuctra. At first, the Athenians, Demosthenes himself among the ranks, staged an enthusiastic charge, as they had at Marathon. But the power of the Macedonian phalanx and Philip's superior battle tactics turned this attack into a retreat. Meanwhile, eighteen-year-old Alexander led the Macedonian cavalry against the Sacred Band, which soon became surrounded. While the Athenians fled in disarray from the battlefield, the Thebans proudly held their ground and died to the last man, like the Spartans at Thermopy-

lae. Philip's decisive victory over the two leading Greek poleis gave him what he had dreamed of for so long—mastery of all Greece.

Pursuing a Glorious Destiny

Philip realized that keeping so many Greek cities under control would not be easy. He could make this task easier, he reasoned, by providing a common enemy for all Greeks to oppose. So, in 337 in Corinth, he assembled representatives from the Greek cities and proposed a united Greek invasion of Persia to avenge the Persian invasion of Greece in the previous century. Having little choice, the Greeks agreed and Philip began preparations for the invasion. The following year, however, he was assassinated. The identity of the murderer remains uncertain, but many Greeks suspected that Alexander and his mother, Olympias, arranged the

Philip is murdered with a Celtic sword in the theater at Pella, Macedonia's capital.

assassination. Philip had recently divorced Olympias, remarried, and had a new son. Both Olympias and Alexander were no doubt worried that Philip might disinherit Alexander in favor of his new half-brother.

At the age of twenty, Alexander took his father's place as leader of Macedonia and Greece. He continued preparations for the Persian expedition, boldly sending the Persian king, Darius III, the warning: "I, Alexander, consider the whole of thy treasure, and the whole of thy land to be mine." In 334, the young king led an army of thirty-two thousand infantry and five thousand cavalry eastward across the Hellespont.

Before proceeding into Asia, Alexander stopped at the legendary site of Troy to pray to the Greek gods for victory in the coming campaign. Troy was a special place for him because he saw himself as a Homeric hero reborn, a new Achilles carrying on the war between West and East. For Alexander, the conquest of Persia was not just a practical move, as it had been for his father. He believed that he was part god himself and that it was his destiny to conquer and rule men. Aristotle had taught him always to seek *arete,* the attainment of personal excellence and glorious deeds. And now the young conqueror intended to accomplish that goal, no matter how difficult the struggle. "It is those who endure toil and who dare dangers," he said, "that achieve glorious deeds; and it is a lovely thing to live with courage, and to die, leaving behind an everlasting renown."[72]

Destroyer and Builder

Between 334 and 331, Alexander led his army to victory after victory over the Per-

Alexander directs the siege of Tyre. Catapults, archers, and slingers assault the defenders manning the city's battlements.

sians and captured the entire eastern section of the Persian Empire. First, the Greeks defeated Darius's armies at Granicus and Issus, both in Asia Minor. Then, Alexander marched southward into Palestine and besieged the island city of Tyre on the Mediterranean coast. The city held out for seven months but finally fell when the Greeks built an earthen causeway from the mainland to the island. In 332, Alexander entered Egypt. After enduring Persian rule for two centuries, the Egyptians welcomed the young general as their liberator and the Greeks won the country without a fight.

Alexander and his troops visit the great Sphinx at Gizeh after liberating Egypt from the Persians.

While in Egypt, Alexander showed that he was not merely a conqueror and destroyer. A lover of knowledge and Greek culture, he sought to spread Greek, or Hellenic, language, arts, ideas, and customs throughout the lands he defeated. This process of Hellenization, he believed, would help unify the many foreign peoples in his new and growing Greek empire. Everywhere he went, Alexander built temples, theaters, gymnasiums, and even whole cities. In 331, near the mouth of the Nile River, he founded a new city, naming

it Alexandria, after himself. According to the ancient historian Arrian:

> The position seemed to him a very fine one in which to found a city. . . . He marked out the boundaries . . . himself, pointing out where the marketplace was to be constructed, where the temples were to be built, stating how many there were to be, and to what Greek gods they were to be dedicated. . . . [The Egyptian priests] told Alexander that the city would become prosperous in every respect.[73]

The priests' prediction proved accurate. In time, Alexandria became one of the greatest commercial and cultural centers in the ancient world.

The Fall of Persia

From Egypt, Alexander turned northeastward in the fall of 331 to resume his conquest of Persia. His expanded army now numbered 40,000 infantry and 7,000 cavalry. Hearing that the Greeks were approaching Babylon, one of Persia's three capitals, Darius assembled an army of at least 250,000 troops at Gaugamela, near the Tigris River in what is now Iraq. There, on October 1, 331, the two forces met in the battle that would forever decide the fate of Persia. Part of Darius's plan was to charge with hundreds of chariots armed with scythes, which are razor-sharp knives, protruding from the wheel hubs. These, he hoped, would cut many of the Greek infantrymen to pieces. But Alexander's troops showered arrows and javelins onto the chariot drivers and horses, halting the charge. Then, wrote Plutarch, the Greek cavalry

> charged at full speed and the phalanx rushed on like a torrent. Before the first ranks [of the armies] were well engaged the barbarians gave way, and Alexander pressed hard . . . in order to penetrate into the midst of the host where Darius himself was, for he beheld him at a distance. . . . A numerous body of select cavalry stood in close order about [Darius's] chariot and seemed well prepared to receive the enemy. But Alexander's approach appeared so terrible . . . the greatest part of them dispersed [fled]. . . . Darius now saw the most dreadful dangers before his eyes. His own forces . . . were driven back upon him; the wheels of his chariot were. . . . entangled among the dead bodies. . . . He quitted the chariot . . . and fled . . . upon a mare [horse].[74]

Learning of Darius's flight, the Persians, far less disciplined than the Greeks, turned and retreated in mass confusion. Alexander's forces gave chase for many hours, slaughtering all those they caught. At least 40,000 Persians perished, while the Greeks lost fewer than 1,000 men.

After the battle, Alexander marched to Babylon, which, after learning the outcome of Gaugamela, opened its gates without a fight. The Greeks then moved on to the other Persian capitals, Susa and Persepolis, where they also met no resistance. Alexander burned Persepolis in 330 and afterward continued his pursuit of Darius. When Alexander finally caught up with Darius, he was dismayed to find that the Persian king had been murdered by Bessus, a Persian satrap, or governor, attempting to win Alexander's favor. Believing that a king should die only in battle or at the hands of another king, Alexander had Bessus executed. Plutarch recalled that Alexander "caused two straight trees to be bent and one of his [Bessus's] legs to

This seventeenth century engraving depicts Alexander's decisive defeat of the Indian monarch Porus, whose forces included 130 elephants.

be fastened to each; then when the trees were returned to their former position, his body was torn asunder by the violence of the recoil."[75]

Alexander's Legacy

Now master of Persia, Alexander decided to continue his eastward trek and further expand his new empire. In the next four years, he marched his army thousands of miles, through what is now Iran, Afghanistan, and Pakistan. All along the way, he established new cities and military forts. In 326, the Greeks reached India and defeated the army of Porus, an Indian prince. Alexander wanted to keep moving eastward into Asia, but his troops, weary of years of travel and fighting, refused to go on. So, Alexander reluctantly led them back to Persia.

There, he continued Hellenizing the Persians, trying various means of merging their culture with that of the Greeks. In one such attempt, he ordered ten thousand of his troops to marry Persian women in one mass ceremony. He also began drawing his plans for further conquests, talking openly about expeditions into Arabia and the Mediterranean. But he never had a chance to implement any of these plans. At the height of his power, Alexander suddenly fell ill, possibly of malaria, and died at the age of thirty-three. As he lay dying, his generals asked to whom he planned to leave his empire. "To the strongest," he replied.[76]

In just ten years, Alexander had created the largest empire the world had seen up to that time. It stretched from Macedonia and Greece in the west to Egypt in the south to India in the east and encompassed more than one million square miles. But

Alexander gazes at the body of his enemy, King Darius. Earlier, a Macedonian soldier named Polystratus had found the wounded monarch and given him water before he died.

To Live with Courage and Die in Glory

In 326 B.C., Alexander the Great reached the Beas River in India and faced the prospect of doing battle with an Indian army with a reputation for strength and bravery. After marching thousands of miles into Asia and fighting many battles, Alexander's troops were weary and reluctant to face this new threat. He summoned his chief officers and, in the manner of a great orator, explained why they should go on. His speech, quoted by Roman historian Arrian in The Anabasis of Alexander, *not only shows his skills of persuasion but also clearly reveals his own obsession with duty, fame, and especially glory:*

"I observe that you, Macedonians and allied forces, are not following me into dangers any longer with your old spirit. I have summoned you together, either to persuade you to go forward or to be persuaded by you and turn back. . . . It is those who endure toil and who dare dangers that achieve glorious deeds; and it is a lovely thing to live with courage, and to die, leaving behind an everlasting renown. . . . If then while you were bearing labors and bearing dangers I had led you, myself, your leader, without labors and without dangers, you would not unnaturally have become weary in your hearts; when you alone had all the labors, and were procuring the prizes thereof for others; but it is not so; our labors are shared in common; we bear an equal part in dangers; the prizes are open to all. For the land is yours . . . and when we master all Asia, then—by Heaven!—I will not merely satisfy you . . . I will send home all who desire to go home or will myself lead them back; those who stay, I shall make to be envied by those who go back."

Alexander reluctantly abandoned India in 326 B.C.

On his deathbed, Alexander feebly watches as his troops bid him farewell. His last prophetic words were, "I foresee a great funeral contest over me."

this vast political unit soon began to fall apart. Shortly after Alexander's death, his generals began fighting each other for control of the Greek empire. Eventually, it would be divided among them. Even though Alexander's empire did not last, the seeds of Greek culture he planted did. Greek language, arts, architecture, and science flourished in Alexandria and other cities he built or Hellenized. Writers and artists in these cities helped pass the torch of Greek culture to later civilizations. Because of this achievement, historian James Henry Breasted remarked, "Alexander has been well termed 'the Great.' Few men of genius—certainly in so brief a career—have left so indelible [lasting] a mark upon the course of human affairs."[77] Thus, Alexander's dream of "everlasting renown" was fulfilled.

Chapter

8 The Hellenistic Age: The Decline of the Greeks

In the three centuries following Alexander's death, Greek civilization experienced its last important phase of independent political and military power. This period is referred to as the Hellenistic Age. The vast empire the Greeks had acquired in a mere decade split into three kingdoms, ruled by the heirs of Alexander's generals. Because they carried on vigorous trade and commercial activities, these kingdoms often enjoyed considerable economic prosperity. But they were repeatedly wracked by rebellions and wars, so in time they grew weaker and more disorganized. Finally, one by one, they fell before the power of Rome, an Italian city whose expanding empire would one day surpass that of Alexander in size and glory.

But while Greek political power declined, Greek culture, vigorously promoted by the rulers of the Greek kingdoms, flourished. Greek literature, arts, philosophy, and religion exerted a profound influence over the peoples of southern Europe, the Middle East, Egypt, and eventually even Rome itself. Nearly everywhere, builders copied Greek architecture. Greek became a universal language, spoken by tens of millions of non-Greeks. Greek historians recorded the events of many lands and peoples, and Greek inventors and scientists used logic and reason to explore the mysteries of nature.

The Successor Kingdoms

The brief period of Greek unity created by Philip and Alexander ended with Alexander's death. Almost immediately, a bloody power struggle among several of Alexander's generals began. Called the *Diadochi,* or "successors," they included Antipater, Cratarus, Antigonus, Perdiccas, Seleucus, Eumenes, and Ptolemy. Between 323 and 281, they fought a long series of costly wars that killed hundreds of thousands of people

Alexander's general, Ptolemy, who ascended the Egyptian throne as Ptolemy Soter, the "preserver."

Scholars study scrolls in the great library at Alexandria. The word "volume" comes from volumina, *meaning scrolls.*

and exhausted all of the participants. The Greek historian Nymphis witnessed some of the fighting that involved his hometown of Heraclea, on the southern coast of the Black Sea:

> Antigonus . . . attempted to reach Macedonia with an army and a fleet before Ptolemy arrived. But Ptolemy intercepted him with . . . ships, and offered battle. There were other ships and also some sent from Heraclea. . . . There was one . . . called the Leontophorus which was much admired for its size and beauty. In this ship 100 men rowed in each bank [level], so that there were 800 of them on each side. . . . When battle was joined Ptolemy prevailed [won], turning back the fleet of Antigonus.[78]

In 281, three kingdoms emerged from the *Diadochi* wars. The first, the Ptolemaic kingdom, ruled by Ptolemy's successors, consisted of Egypt and nearby southern Palestine. The Ptolemies did not attempt to impose a Greek-style oligarchy or democracy in Egypt. Instead, they took the Egyptian title of pharaoh and maintained the absolute monarchy that had existed in the country for centuries. Alexandria became the greatest trade and commercial center of the age, enabling the Egyptian nobility and upper classes to enjoy great wealth and luxury.

The Seleucid kingdom, ruled by the descendants of Seleucus, consisted of the lands north of the Persian Gulf—the heart of the old Persian Empire—and parts of Asia Minor. Seleucus and his son, Antiochus I, set up many independent cities using the Greek polis as a model. These cities were allowed to decide their own local affairs. But they also had to pay heavy taxes to and obey the orders and whims of the Seleucids, who were absolute monarchs like the Ptolemies. The Seleucid city of Antioch, located on the eastern Mediterranean coast, grew large and prosperous and became the commercial rival of Alexandria.

The Macedonian kingdom was the third large political unit. Consisting of Macedonia and Greece, it was ruled by the heirs of Antigonus. The Antigonids, like the Seleucids, allowed individual poleis a certain measure of self-rule but also exerted ultimate kingly authority. The Antigonids encountered many difficulties. First, they found it hard to govern the Greeks, who were still fiercely independent and always rebelling. Also, in 280, the Gauls, a semicivilized tribal people from central Europe, invaded Greece. The warlike Gauls swept through the country, killing, burning, and looting. According to the Greek traveler and geographer Pausanias:

> They butchered all the males, and likewise old women, and babes at their mothers' breasts; they drank the blood, and feasted on the flesh of infants that were fat. High-spirited women and maidens . . . committed suicide . . . those that survived were subjected to every kind of outrage. . . . Some of the women rushed upon the swords of the Gauls. . . . To others death came from absence of food or sleep, as these merciless barbarians ravished them in turn, and wreaked their lusts upon [raped] them whether dying or dead.[79]

In 277, after three years of desperate fighting, Antigonus II, grandson of the kingdom's founder, managed to drive the invaders out and restore order. But the peace

The early Gauls were part of vast migrations of nomadic peoples from central Asia into Europe.

did not last long. In the following decades, Macedonia, like the other two Greek kingdoms, had to deal with internal rebellions by subjects unhappy with their dictatorial rulers. And each kingdom continued to fight periodic wars with its neighbors.

Commerce and Culture

During all this fighting, a major economic transformation took place in the Mediterranean world. Before Alexander's death, Athens had been the commercial leader of the Mediterranean for more than a century. But as the Ptolemaic and Seleucid kingdoms gained prominence, the center of trade shifted to Alexandria and Antioch. Athens and most of the other mainland Greek poleis underwent a significant economic decline. Unable to make ends meet, many people left Athens or had fewer children, so the population also declined. The Greek historian Polybius reported, "In our time the whole of Greece has been subject to a low birth rate and a general decrease of population, owing to which cities have become deserted and the land has ceased to yield fruit."[80] By the second century B.C., living standards in Greece were noticeably lower than in previous centuries. Visiting Athens in the early second century, the Greek traveler Heracleides Creticus noted: "The city is quite dry and poorly watered, while because it is so old the arrangement of the streets is bad. Most of the houses are shabby though there are a few respectable ones. A stranger seeing it for the first time might refuse to believe that this was the famous city of Athens."[81]

By contrast, Alexandria was a new and prosperous center of trade, commerce, and learning. Its population constantly increased during the Hellenistic period, eventually reaching almost one million. This was partly because people from many other cities and countries found its modern, cosmopolitan atmosphere attractive. The Greek writer Herodas said of Alexandria, "Everything is to be found there—wealth, playgrounds, a large army, a serene sky, public displays, philosophers, precious metals, fine young men, a good royal house, an academy of science, exquisite wines, and beautiful women."[82] Antioch, with a population in the Seleucid years of about 600,000 people, was nearly as prosperous as Alexandria and equally cosmopolitan.

These and other important Hellenistic cities were also cultural centers in which many non-Greeks adopted Greek customs, language, and architecture. All government functions, banking, and official affairs utilized the Greek language, which was also taught in all schools. As a result, Greek eventually became the language of the wealthy and educated classes. The Jews of Alexandria translated the Bible from Hebrew into Greek so that educated Jews could read it. Many common people also spoke Greek, although few of them could read or write it.

The great Pharos at Alexandria as it appeared in the first century B.C. It was built in 280 B.C. by the Greek architect Sostratos of Cnidus.

Greek architecture was widely admired and copied. Before the Hellenistic Age, most of the great Greek public buildings had been temples, such as the Parthenon. Hellenistic architects and builders adopted Greek temple styles to government buildings and libraries, which were often located in the center of a city. Sometimes, the architects incorporated features and details from Egyptian, Persian, or other kinds of buildings, creating stunning new Greek-like styles. One of the most famous and impressive buildings constructed during the Hellenistic Age was the Pharos, a stone lighthouse that stood in Alexandria's harbor. Reaching a height of 445 feet, or thirty-six stories, it was the world's first skyscraper. The Pharos was so well built that it lasted for more than fifteen hundred years, finally falling during an earthquake in the 1300s.

Hipparchus, seen marking the position of a star, drew up the first known star catalog.

I Will Move the World

Of the other aspects of Greek culture and learning that thrived in Hellenistic times, the advancement of science is perhaps the most impressive. For example, in the early third century B.C., Aristarchus of Samos built upon the ideas of former Greek astronomers. He began with the notion that the earth is a sphere, which Greek scientists had known for at least a century. It remains uncertain who first suggested it, but Aristotle accepted the idea as fact, writing shortly before the beginning of the Hellenistic Age: "The sphericity of the earth is proved by the evidence of our senses, for otherwise lunar eclipses would not take such forms. . . . In eclipses the dividing line [between light and dark on the moon's face] is always rounded. Consequently, if the eclipse is due to the interposition of the earth [between sun and moon], the rounded line results from its spherical shape."[83] Aristarchus suggested that the other planets are spheres like the earth and moon. Furthermore, he said, the earth does not rest at the center of the universe, as people had always believed. He proposed that the sun, much larger than the earth, is at the center, and that the earth and planets revolve around it.

Later, in the second century B.C., another Greek astronomer, Hipparchus of Nicaea, rejected the sun-centered universe in favor of the earth-centered theory. Hipparchus, however, made many brilliant and correct astronomical discoveries and calculations. He measured the distance from the earth to the moon with an error of only 5 percent. He also invented the system of lines of longitude and latitude for use on maps of both the sky and the earth.

The greatest scientist and inventor of the period was Archimedes, who lived in Syracuse in the third century B.C. One of his most famous discoveries came one day when he was sitting in a bathtub. As he and countless others had noticed before, when he submerged himself, the water level rose and his body appeared to weigh less. Suddenly, Archimedes deduced why this occurs. A floating body, he realized, loses weight in direct proportion to the weight of the water it displaces. This later became known as the principle of buoyancy.

Archimedes also experimented with new ways to make physical labor easier. In one of his most celebrated demonstrations, he had a large dry-docked ship loaded with supplies and people. To the ship he attached ropes that ran to a complicated mechanism made up of pulleys and levers. Operating this device alone, he succeeded in lifting the ship into the air and placing it undamaged in the water. Afterward, he reportedly boasted, "Give me a place to stand on and I will move the world."

Archimedes designed similar large-scale mechanical devices for use in warfare and actually tested some. When the Romans attacked Syracuse in 212, he used huge cranes and hooks to lift enemy ships out of the water and capsize them. He also designed large catapults that slung heavy rocks at advancing Roman ships and soldiers. The effect of these inventions was devastating. Polybius wrote: "Such a great and marvelous thing does the genius of one man show itself to be when properly applied. The Romans, strong both by sea and by land, had every

Archimedes, holding his compass, was the first to calculate the mathematical value of pi.

hope of capturing the town at once if one old man of Syracuse [Archimedes] were removed; as long as he was present they did not venture to attack."[84]

The Last Gasps of Culture and Power

Throughout most of his long life, Archimedes stayed in touch with his colleagues in Alexandria, where he had studied as a young man. There, Greek scientists worked and experimented in a university known as the Museum. Generously supported by the

Measuring the World

Eratosthenes was one of the greatest scientists and scholars of the Hellenistic period and, indeed, of all antiquity. He is best known for his work in geography and astronomy. Like other Greek scientists at the time, Eratosthenes was well aware that the earth is a sphere. But how big a sphere? As Will Durant explained:

"[Eratosthenes'] greatest achievement was his calculation of the earth's circumference as 24,662 miles; we compute it [in modern times] at 24,847. Observing that at noon on the summer solstice the sun at Syene [in Egypt] shone directly upon the deep surface of a narrow well, and learning that at the same moment the shadow of an obelisk at Alexandria, some five hundred miles north, showed the sun to be approximately 7½° away from the zenith [high point of the sky] as measured on the meridian of longitude [imaginary line] that connected the two cities, he concluded that an arc of 7½° on the earth's circumference equalled five hundred miles, and that the entire circumference would equal 360 ÷ 7.5 x 500, or 24,000 miles."

Ptolemies, it was the world's first government-sponsored scientific institution. The Alexandrian scientists made many important discoveries about the universe, the earth, animals, plants, and human beings. For example, Euclid made important advances in mathematics, especially geometry. Theophrastus described and classified all the plants known in his time, while Herophilus studied human anatomy and discovered the optic nerve that leads from the eye to the brain. And Eratosthenes correctly measured the circumference of the earth.

Unfortunately, most of the great discoveries and writings produced by these scientists did not survive to be passed on to future generations. This was partly because of the skeptical attitudes of political and religious leaders as well as of the general public. Most people simply refused to believe such revolutionary ideas as the sun-centered universe. Also, most of the written works of these scientists were lost. These works, along with earlier Greek scientific, literary, and philosophical writings, were stored in the great Alexandrian library that adjoined the Museum. This library contained an estimated 700,000 works, representing the collected wisdom of many nations and centuries. During later Roman times, the library burned, and most of these writings were destroyed. It would take more than fourteen hundred years for scientists to begin rediscovering much of this lost knowledge.

These scientific endeavors, among the last examples of original Greek thought,

The leading citizens of a Seleucid city, possibly Antioch or Tyre, bow to Roman troops who have captured the town. Seleucid lands in Asia Minor fell to the Romans in 188 B.C.

took place in an era when Greek political and military power was rapidly declining. Beginning in the third century B.C., Rome's mighty armies and navies conquered the nations bordering the Mediterranean one by one. While the researchers at the Museum studied and experimented, they witnessed the last gasps of independent Greek rule. The Macedonian kingdom, including Athens and the other city-states of southern Greece, fell to the Romans by 146 B.C. The Seleucid kingdom held out longer, but it, too, was defeated and became a Roman province in 64. That left only the Ptolemaic kingdom. In 31, the Romans defeated Cleopatra, last of the Ptolemies, and Mark Anthony, her Roman lover, in a great sea battle near Actium on the western coast of Greece. Afterward, Anthony and Cleopatra committed suicide. In the following year, Rome absorbed Egypt.

The fall of the last Greek kingdom marked the closing of one of history's greatest eras. As the Romans became the new masters of the Mediterranean world, Pericles, Alexander, and the many other talented Greeks who had shaped that world settled into the long sleep of eternal fame. The epic two-thousand-year journey of the Greeks at the forefront of Western civilization had reached its end.

Epilogue

The Greek Spirit Lives

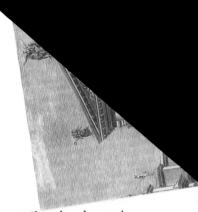

The influence of the Greeks did not end with the decline of their magnificent civilization. Many aspects of Greek culture survived and were passed down through the generations to the modern world. Greek ideas, arts, and theories of government helped shape many of today's societies. "If ever a people changed the face of the world," remarked C. M. Bowra, "it was the Greeks of the sixth and fifth centuries B.C. . . . Without them we should indeed be different from what we are."[85]

Greece's cultural legacy reached the modern world largely via Rome. After conquering the Greeks, the powerful Romans continued to expand their empire until Rome eventually held sway over the entire Mediterranean world, much of southern Europe, northern Africa, and the Middle East. With its large, well-trained armies, Rome was able to control most of this vast territory for several centuries. Though they ruled by force, the Romans were builders rather than destroyers, and they built on a grand scale. The many thousands of roads, theaters, temples, public buildings, baths, and aqueducts they constructed all over their empire were larger and more imposing than any built before. Rome itself became the largest and most splendid city in the ancient world.

One reason for Rome's success was that the Romans were a highly practical and efficient people. Always searching for ways to improve their own system, they often adopted the best aspects of the peoples they conquered. When the Romans subdued Greece and the last Greek kingdoms,

The hilltop Temple of Jupiter, the Roman version of Zeus, dominates this view of ancient Rome.

The Temple of Pallas, like other Roman temples, borrowed the basic Greek design of a triangular pediment atop six columns.

they became enchanted with Greek customs, arts, and ideas and readily copied many of these. Roman writers, for example, openly imitated the styles and themes of Greek literature, and Rome's comic playwrights eagerly adopted Aristophanes' slapstick style. Many of Rome's great public buildings were modeled after Greek temples like the Parthenon. In addition, Roman law and government borrowed many principles from the Greeks. Although Rome never became a true democracy, Greek democratic ideas helped shape the semi-democratic republic that ruled Rome for nearly five centuries.

Later, Rome passed these and many other aspects of Greek culture on to later civilizations. Rome fell in the fifth century A.D., and the impact and influence of Roman culture on European peoples gradually decreased. Then, centuries later, dur-

ing the Renaissance of the 1400s and 1500s, Europeans rediscovered the arts and ideas of the Romans and with them those of the Greeks. European painters, sculptors, architects, poets, and thinkers were profoundly influenced by Greek and Roman "classical" styles. In the three centuries following the Renaissance, Europeans colonized many other parts of the world. In the process, they spread classical ideas, arts, and literature around the globe to new nations that, in turn, absorbed them and passed them on. In this way, Greece's cultural legacy reached the modern world.

Democratic government is one of the most important concepts passed on from ancient Greece. The founders of the United States, for instance, based their new democracy partly on that of ancient Athens. There were important differences, of course. Because of Athens's small population, its citizens could all gather to decide and vote directly on important matters. So Athens had a "direct" democracy. Out of necessity, the much more populous United States became a "representative" democracy, in which one person represents the interests of many others in the decision-making process. For the most part, however, the United States and other modern democracies utilize the basic ideas of freedom and self-rule developed by the Greeks. The modern "democratic idea of a government responsible to the governed," wrote Will Durant, "of trial by jury, and of civil liberties of thought, writing, assemblage, and worship, have been profoundly stimulated by Greek history."[86]

The buildings that house these democratic institutions are also often inspired by Greek models. Greek art, in general, and classical Greek temple architecture, in particular, are often seen as the ideal of artistic symmetry, grace, strength, and beauty. Just as it dominated the great public squares of ancient Rome, Greek architecture also dominates the government buildings of Washington, D.C., and hundreds of other cities across the United States and around the world. The exteriors of thousands of modern courthouses, libraries, and university buildings also bear the familiar rows of Greek columns topped by a triangular pediment. And the interiors of theaters, opera houses, and hotels are frequently adorned with paintings and statues depicting ancient Greek gods and heroes.

Just as Greek architecture is the basis for many modern buildings, the Greek language is a major cornerstone of many modern languages. Several European languages, including French and English, have thousands of root words derived from Greek. Every day, usually without realizing it, people in English-speaking societies use dozens of common Greek words. These include words dealing with government, such as *democracy, politics, tyrant, monarch,* and *despot.* Common Greek words

The National Archives building in Washington, D.C., one of many modern structures designed on Greek models.

describing the entertainment world are *drama, comedy, tragedy, orchestra,* and *harmony.* And the Greeks supplied the words for the branches of learning, including *philosophy, biology, mathematics, geometry, zoology,* and *history.*

Now a decaying ruin, the Temple of Apollo in Bassae, Greece was once as imposing as the structure seen above.

Perhaps the most profound aspect of Greek culture adopted by modern societies is the belief in the worth of the individual. C. M. Bowra said:

> Greek civilization was ultimately made possible by a belief in the special worth of man. The Greeks did not see him as a corrupt and fallen being. . . . They saw that man was indeed an unprecedented creature, worthy of awe and wonder in the scale of his inventions and his enterprises. Sophocles speaks for them when he makes a chorus [in one of his plays] sing: There are many strange wonders, but nothing more wonderful than man.[87]

The belief that each individual is worthy and therefore ought to enjoy certain basic liberties survived. It became the inspiration for the Founding Fathers when they wrote that people are endowed with certain inalienable rights. Among these rights, they stated, are "life, liberty, and the pursuit of happiness." Indeed, said Aristotle, the pursuit of happiness should be a major life goal of the worthy individual. Many people today automatically accept that premise, searching as a matter of course for respect and fulfillment in their jobs, relationships, and community.

In this way, part of the spirit of the ancient Greeks, a people long dead, remains and perhaps always will remain. It is the spirit not only of human worth and freedom but also of the quest for beauty and truth. The Greeks sought to discover and understand the truth about nature and about themselves. It is human destiny to uncover these truths, they believed, because human beings possess the intellec-

Aristotle, who called happiness, "The highest of all practical goods."

tual tools to do so. Chief among these tools, they recognized, is reason, the use of logic to separate good from bad or deduce one fact from another. "Such to man is the life according to reason," said Aristotle, "since it is this that makes him man."[88]

That desire to unlock nature's secrets using reason and logic was what drove Archimedes, Anaxagoras, and the other Greek scientists to their discoveries. And that same desire, passed down through the ages from ancient Greece, fires the dreams and efforts of modern scientists. Today's researchers, like their Greek predecessors, seek to explain the origins and workings of the universe, of life, and of the human mind. As long as people reach out to know, to learn, and to find the truth, the Greek spirit will never die.

Notes

Introduction: A Simple and Noble Concept

1. C. M. Bowra and the editors of Time-Life Books, *Classical Greece*. New York: Time-Life Books, 1965.

2. Charles Alexander Robinson Jr., *Ancient Greece*. New York: Franklin Watts, 1984.

Chapter 1: The Age of Heroes: The Birth of Greek Civilization

3. Robert Payne, *Ancient Greece: The Triumph of a Culture*. New York: W. W. Norton, 1964.

4. Payne, *Ancient Greece: The Triumph of a Culture*.

5. Plutarch, *Lives of the Noble Grecians and Romans*. Translated by John Dreyden. New York: Random House, 1932.

6. Bowra, *Classical Greece*.

7. J. V. Luce, *Lost Atlantis: New Light on an Old Legend*. New York: McGraw-Hill, 1969.

8. Homer, *Iliad*. Translated by E. V. Rieu. Baltimore: Penguin Books, 1950.

9. Stringfellow Barr, *The Will of Zeus: A History of Greece from the Origins of Hellenic Culture to the Death of Alexander*. New York: Dell, 1961.

Chapter 2: The Rise of City-States: Prelude to the Classic Age

10. Bowra, *Classical Greece*.

11. Will Durant, *The Life of Greece*. New York: Simon & Schuster, 1966.

12. Payne, *Ancient Greece: The Triumph of a Culture*.

13. Susan Peach and Anne Millard, *The Greeks*. London: Usborne, 1990.

14. Bowra, *Classical Greece*.

15. Victor Ehrenberg, *From Solon to Socrates: Greek Civilization During the 6th and 5th Centuries B.C.* London: Methuen, 1967.

16. Plutarch, *Lives*.

Chapter 3: West Versus East: The Greek and Persian Wars

17. Herodotus, *The Persian Wars*. Translated by Glanville Downey, in *Stories from Herodotus*. New York: E. P. Dutton, 1965.

18. Herodotus, *The Persian Wars*. Translated by George Rawlinson, in *The Greek Historians*. Edited by Francis R. B. Godolphin. New York: Random House, 1942.

19. Herodotus, *The Persian Wars*. Quoted in Lt. Col. Joseph B. Mitchell and Sir Edward Creasy, *Twenty Decisive Battles of the World*. New York: Macmillan, 1964.

20. Archer Jones, *The Art of War in the Western World*. New York: Oxford University Press, 1987.

21. Herodotus, *The Persian Wars*.

22. Peter Levi, *Atlas of the Greek World*. New York: Facts on File, 1984.

23. Herodotus, *The Persian Wars*.

24. Herodotus, *The Persian Wars*.

25. Herodotus, *The Persian Wars*.

26. Aeschylus, *The Persians*. Quoted in Payne, *Ancient Greece: The Triumph of a Culture*.

27. Durant, *The Life of Greece*.

28. W. G. Hardy, *The Greek and Roman World*. Cambridge, MA: Schenkman, 1962.

Chapter 4: Athenian Empire: Power and Expansion Inflame Old Rivalries

29. Thucydides, *The Peloponnesian Wars*. First published in Greek manuscript circa 400 B.C. Modern edition translated by Benjamin Jowett. New York: Washington Square Press, 1963.

30. Thucydides, *The Peloponnesian Wars*.

31. Quoted in Thucydides, *The Peloponnesian Wars*.

32. Thucydides, *The Peloponnesian Wars*.

33. Plutarch, *Lives*.

34. Quoted in Dorothy Mills, *The Book of the Ancient Greeks: An Introduction to the History and Civilization of Greece from the Coming of the Greeks to the Conquest of Corinth by Rome in 146 B.C.* New York: G. P. Putnam's Sons, 1925.

35. Thucydides, *The Peloponnesian Wars*.

36. Hardy, *The Greek and Roman World*.

37. Plutarch, *Lives*.

38. Payne, *Ancient Greece: The Triumph of a Culture*.

39. Pericles, *Funeral Oration*. Quoted in Bowra, *Classical Greece*.

40. Pericles, *Funeral Oration*. Quoted in Perry Scott King, *Pericles*. New York: Chelsea House, 1988.

Chapter 5: Cultural Outburst: The Golden Age of Athens

41. Quoted in Bowra, *Classical Greece*.

42. C. E. Robinson, *Everyday Life in Ancient Greece*. Oxford, England: Clarendon Press, 1933.

43. Peach and Millard, *The Greeks*.

44. Xenophon, *The Economist*. Quoted in Mills, *The Book of the Ancient Greeks*.

45. Pericles, *Funeral Oration*. Quoted in Robinson, *Everyday Life in Ancient Greece*.

46. Plutarch, *Lives*.

47. Lycurgus, *Against Leocrates*. Quoted in Durant, *The Life of Greece*.

48. Quoted in Durant, *The Life of Greece*.

49. Plato, *The Apology*. Quoted in Paul J. Alexander, ed., *The Ancient World: To 300 A.D.* New York: Macmillan, 1963.

50. Plutarch, *Life of Pericles*. Quoted in Peter Green, *The Parthenon*. New York: Newsweek Book Division, 1973.

51. Quoted in Green, *The Parthenon*.

52. Durant, *The Life of Greece*.

53. Sophocles, *Antigone*. Quoted in Durant, *The Life of Greece*.

54. Aristophanes, *Clouds*. Translated by Jack Lindsay, in *The Complete Plays of Aristophanes*. Edited by Moses Hadas. New York: Bantam Books, 1962.

55. Anaxagoras, quoted in Durant, *The Life of Greece*.

56. Pericles, *Funeral Oration*.

57. Edith Hamilton, *The Greek Way to Western Civilization*. New York: New American Library, 1942.

Chapter 6: Greek Versus Greek: The Peloponnesian War

58. Thucydides, *The Peloponnesian Wars*.

59. Speech of the Corinthians, quoted in Thucydides, *The Peloponnesian Wars*.

60. Thucydides, *The Peloponnesian Wars*.

61. Thucydides, *The Peloponnesian Wars*.

62. Thucydides, *The Peloponnesian Wars*.

63. Plutarch, *Lives*.

64. Plutarch, *Lives*.

65. Thucydides, *The Peloponnesian Wars*.

66. Thucydides, *The Peloponnesian Wars*.

67. Xenophon, *Hellenica*. Quoted in Mills, *The Book of the Ancient Greeks*.

Chapter 7: Alexander's Conquests: The Spread of Greek Culture

68. Plutarch, *Lives.*

69. Aristotle, *Politics.* Quoted in Barr, *The Will of Zeus.*

70. Demosthenes, *First Philippic.* Quoted in Bowra, *Classical Greece.*

71. Alexander of Macedon, quoted in Mills, *The Book of the Ancient Greeks.*

72. Arrian, *Anabasis of Alexander.* Quoted in Barr, *The Will of Zeus.*

73. Arrian, *Anabasis of Alexander.*

74. Plutarch, *Lives.*

75. Plutarch, *Lives.*

76. Alexander of Macedon, quoted in Arrian, *Anabasis of Alexander.*

77. James Henry Breasted, *Ancient Times: A History of the Early World.* Boston: Ginn, 1944.

Chapter 8: The Hellenistic Age: The Decline of the Greeks

78. Nymphis of Heraclea quoted in Memnon, *History of Heraclea,* in *Sources of Western Civilization: Ancient Greece.* Edited by Truesdell S. Brown. New York: Macmillan, 1965.

79. Pausanias, *Description of Greece.* Quoted in Durant, *The Life of Greece.*

80. Polybius, *Histories.* Quoted in Durant, *The Life of Greece.*

81. Heracleides Creticus, *Notes on the Greek Cities.* Quoted in Brown, *Sources of Western Civilization: Ancient Greece.*

82. Herodas, *Mimiambi.* Quoted in Durant, *The Life of Greece.*

83. Aristotle, *Physics.* Quoted in Daniel Boorstin, *The Discoverers: A History of Man's Search to Know His World and Himself.* New York: Random House, 1983.

84. Polybius, *Histories.*

Epilogue: The Greek Spirit Lives On

85. Bowra, *Classical Greece.*

86. Durant, *The Life of Greece.*

87. C. M. Bowra, *The Greek Experience.* New York: New American Library, 1957.

88. Aristotle, quoted in Hamilton, *The Greek Way to Western Civilization.*

For Further Reading

Isaac Asimov, *The Greeks: A Great Adventure.* Boston: Houghton Mifflin, 1965. Excellent, entertaining overview of the ancient Greeks, with an emphasis on their importance to later cultures. Written for advanced readers.

David Bellingham, *An Introduction to Greek Mythology.* Secaucus, NJ: Chartwell Books, 1989. Explains the major Greek myths and legends and their importance to the ancient Greeks. Contains many beautiful photos and drawings.

C. M. Bowra and the editors of Time-Life Books, *Classical Greece.* New York: Time-Life Books, 1965. Excellent presentation of ancient Greek history, culture, and thought with many excellent photos.

Peter Connolly, *The Legend of Odysseus.* New York: Oxford University Press, 1986. Excellent, easy-to-read summary of the events of Homer's *Odyssey,* including many informative sidebars about the way people lived in Mycenaean times. Also contains many marvelous illustrations of the fortresses, homes, ships, and armor of the period.

Editors of Time-Life Books, *A Soaring Spirit: Time Frame 600–400 B.C.* Alexandria, VA: Time-Life Books, 1987. Discusses the Greek wars with Persia and the splendor of Athenian culture, while explaining the rise of the ancient Roman and Chinese cultures that occurred during the same period. Contains many fine photos and maps.

Homer, *Iliad.* Retold by Barbara Leonie Picard. New York: Oxford University Press, 1960; and Homer, *Odyssey.* Retold by Barbara Leonie Picard. New York: Oxford University Press, 1952. Simple, entertaining versions of the classic tales, translated and presented specifically for young readers.

John Ellis Jones, *History as Evidence: Ancient Greece.* New York: Warwick Press, 1983. Introduction to ancient Greece for basic readers. Covers mainly Mycenae, Athens, Olympia, and Delos. Contains numerous photos and drawings.

Magnus Magnusson, *Introducing Archaeology.* New York: Henry Z. Walck, 1972. The story of digging for vanished civilizations, told simply. Includes the classic expeditions of Heinrich Schliemann at Mycenae and Sir Arthur Evans at Knossos on Crete.

Susan Peach and Anne Millard, *The Greeks.* London: Usborne, 1990. A general overview of the history, culture, and myths of ancient Greece for basic readers. Filled with excellent color illustrations.

Charles Alexander Robinson Jr., *Ancient Greece.* New York: Franklin Watts, 1984. Easy-to-read but very general summary of ancient Greek history.

Michael Wood, *In Search of the Trojan War.* New York: New American Library, 1985. A fascinating and well-researched account of the various archaeologists and expeditions that have worked at Troy. Tells how Heinrich Schliemann and others proved that the events of Homer's *Iliad* were true and includes some excellent reconstructions showing what the city looked like in its prime.

Peter Young, ed., *The War Game.* London: Cassell, 1972. In addition to a detailed, exciting account of the battle of Thermopylae by historian Charles Grant, this volume contains fascinating descriptions of other important battles from history, including Agincourt, Waterloo, and Gettysburg.

Works Consulted

Paul J. Alexander, ed., *The Ancient World: To 300 A.D.* New York: Macmillan, 1963. Selections of ancient literature, translated into English with scholarly commentary.

Isaac Asimov, *The Greeks: A Great Adventure.* Boston: Houghton Mifflin, 1965. Well-researched and nicely written overview covering the entire sweep of ancient Greek civilization from Minoan times to the Greek scientists at Alexandria.

C. M. Bowra, *The Greek Experience.* New York: New American Library, 1957. An excellent general discussion of ancient Greek history and culture by a fine historian and writer.

James Henry Breasted, *Ancient Times: A History of the Early World.* New York: Ginn, 1944. Somewhat dated but still masterful and concisely written account of ancient history by one of the great historians of the twentieth century.

A. R. Burn, *Persia and the Greeks: The Defense of the West, 546–478 B.C.* London: Edward Arnold, 1962. Well-researched account of the Greek and Persian wars, with an emphasis on their importance to later European culture.

Will Durant, *The Life of Greece.* New York: Simon & Schuster, 1966. A detailed, scholarly study of all aspects of Greek civilization, with special emphasis placed on the various aspects of everyday life, attitudes, and beliefs.

Michael Grant, *The Classical Greeks.* New York: Charles Scribner's Sons, 1989. A collection of short but highly informative biographies of some of the most important figures in Greek history, including Themistocles, Cimon, Aeschylus, Pericles, Herodotus, Socrates, Plato, and Philip of Macedon.

Michael Grant, *The Rise of the Greeks.* New York: Macmillan, 1987. A highly detailed, scholarly study of early Greek civilization, focusing mainly on the formation of city-states during the dark age.

Peter Green, *Alexander the Great.* New York: Praeger, 1970. Effective general overview of Alexander's conquests, written for the general public.

Peter Green, *Alexander of Macedon, 356–323 B.C.: A Historical Biography.* Berkeley: University of California Press, 1991. An extremely detailed, scholarly study of Alexander and his father, Philip of Macedon, with an emphasis on the political intrigues of Macedon and other Greek states at the time. More advanced reading than Green's earlier book *Alexander the Great.*

Edith Hamilton, *The Greek Way to Western Civilization.* New York: New American Library, 1942. In one of the modern classic books about the Greeks, Hamilton explores the contributions of the Greeks to the world's art, literature, and philosophy. She explains what made the Greeks unique: their logical and refreshing view of human beings and their place in the scheme of things. A beautifully written and moving book.

Edith Hamilton, *Mythology.* New York: New American Library, 1940. Hamilton's excellent telling of the Greek myths is still considered the best and most entertaining overview of its kind.

W. G. Hardy, *The Greek and Roman World.* Cambridge, MA: Schenkman, 1962. A brief but effective overview of Greek culture, with an emphasis on everyday life, Athenian democracy, and philosophy.

Archer Jones, *The Art of War in the Western World.* New York: Oxford University Press, 1987. A scholarly study of the weapons and techniques of warfare in history. Contains excellent, detailed descriptions of ancient Greek hoplites, Greek phalanx and other battle formations, and important battle sites such as Marathon, Plataea, and Issus.

Donald Kagan, *The Outbreak of the Peloponnesian War.* Ithaca, NY: Cornell University Press, 1969. A scholarly examination of the causes of one of the most important wars in human history.

Perry Scott King, *Pericles.* New York: Chelsea House, 1988. Short but nicely researched and well-written biography of the man who led Athens during its golden age.

H. D. F. Kitto, *The Greeks.* Baltimore: Penguin Books, 1951. One of the best overviews of ancient Greece, written by an acknowledged expert in the field.

Peter Levi, *Atlas of the Greek World.* New York: Facts on File, 1984. A handsome edition that provides an overview of Greek civilization, with many maps, color photos, drawings, and interesting sidebars about art and customs.

Eduard C. Lindeman, ed., *Life Stories of Men Who Shaped History from Plutarch's* Lives. New York: New American Library, 1950. A fine translation of Plutarch's *Lives,* including his fascinating and informative descriptions of Pericles, Alcibiades, and Alexander the Great.

James W. Mavor Jr., *Voyage to Atlantis.* New York: G. P. Putnam's Sons, 1969. A fascinating description of the excavations on the Greek island of Thera (Santorini), revealing the lost Minoan city of Akrotiri and how it was destroyed by the volcanic eruption that took place on the island about 1500 B.C. Explains how the legend of Atlantis, as described by Plato, was a dim memory of the destruction of ancient Thera.

Lt. Col. Joseph B. Mitchell and Sir Edward Creasy, *Twenty Decisive Battles of the World.* New York: Macmillan, 1964. A classic study of history's most strategic battles, including those at Marathon, Syracuse, and Guagamela.

Claude Mosse, *Athens in Decline, 404–86 B.C.* London: Routledge & Kegan Paul, 1973. Detailed, scholarly study of Athens after its defeat in the Peloponnesian War.

Gilbert Murray, *The Literature of Ancient Greece.* Chicago: University of Chicago Press, 1956. Informative overview of and commentary about Greek literature, including a discussion of Homer, Herodotus, Thucydides, the great dramatists, Xenophon, Demosthenes, and others.

Robert Payne, *Ancient Greece: The Triumph of a Culture.* New York: W. W. Norton, 1964. Very well written and entertaining general study of ancient Greek civilization.

Charles Pellegrino, *Unearthing Atlantis: An Archaeological Odyssey.* New York: Random House, 1991. Well-researched and extremely informative overview of the excavations on the island of Thera, Minoan culture and art, and the connection of the great Thera eruption with the legend of Atlantis.

Charles Alexander Robinson Jr., *Athens in the Age of Pericles.* Norman: University of Oklahoma Press, 1959. A detailed look at everyday life in Athens during Greece's golden age, with plenty of discussion of Greek democracy and politics, as well as descriptions of art, drama, and sculpture.

Thucydides, *The Peloponnesian Wars.* First published circa 400 B.C. Modern edition translated by Benjamin Jowett. New York: Washington Square Press, 1963. Even after more than two thousand years, master historian Thucydides' account of the wars that ended Greece's golden age remains colorful, riveting reading. Highly recommended for all.

Emily Vermeule, *Greece in the Bronze Age.* Chicago: University of Chicago Press, 1972. Excellent, detailed study of early Greek culture, told by one of the greatest of modern historians.

T. B. L. Webster, *From Mycenae to Homer.* New York: W. W. Norton, 1964. A highly detailed, scholarly study of early Greek literature and art. Best approached with a prior knowledge of early Greek civilization.

Index

Achilles, 19, 20, 81
acropolis, 23
　Athenian, 22, 40, 42, 54
　　rebuilding of, 60–61, 63
Aeschylus, 11, 42–43, 62
Agamemnon, 18, 19
Age of Heroes, 12, 25, 62
Ajax, 19
Alcibiades, 60, 70
　betrayal of Athens, 72, 73
　Plutarch's description of,
　　71, 72
Alexander the Great, 76
　battles of
　　at Chaeronea, 80
　　at Gaugamela, 82–83
　　in India, 83, 84, 85
　　in Persian Empire, 81,
　　　82–83
　death of, 84, 86
　division of empire of,
　　87–89
　education of, 78–79
　in Egypt, 81–82
　on glory, 85
Alexander the Great (Green), 78
Alexandria, Egypt
　building of, 82
　influence of, 88, 89, 90
　library at, 88, 93
　university at (Museum),
　　92–93, 94
Anaxagoras, 51, 65, 98
*Ancient Times: A History of the
　Early World* (Breasted),
　46
Annals of Alexander, The
　(Arrian), 85
Anthony, Mark, 94
Antigone (Sophocles), 63
Antigonus, 87, 88
Antigonus II, 89
Antioch, 88, 89, 90, 94
Antiochus I, 88
Antipater, 87
Aphrodite, 25

Apollo, 25, 26, 27
archaeological excavations
　of Crete, 13, 14
　of Troy, 19, 21
Archidamus, 68
Archimedes, 92, 98
architecture
　Greek
　　columns, 56, 97
　　during Hellenistic Age,
　　　90, 91
　　influence of, 87, 96–97
　　Parthenon, 40, 42,
　　　60–61, 63, 96
　　using slave labor, 57
　Minoan, 12
　Roman, 95, 96
　see also temples
arete, 81
Argos, 28
Ariadne, 14
Aristarchus of Samos, 91
Aristophanes, 62, 64, 96
Aristotle, 78, 81
　on astronomy, 91
　philosophy of, 79, 98
Arrian, 82, 85
art, 87
　honoring athletes, 27, 29
　Minoan, 12, 14
　pottery, 16, 27, 55, 56, 59
　revival after dark ages, 28
　rulers' support for, 30, 54
　sculpture, 24, 25, 40, 50,
　　57, 61, 62, 63
　spread of Greek, 96–97
Artemis, 25
Asia Minor, 18, 21, 28, 88, 94
Aspasia, 58
Assyria, 33
astronomy, 65, 91–92, 93
Athena, 19, 40, 50, 61, 63
Athens, 21, 28
　contacts with Minoans, 13,
　　14, 15
　decline of, 89

economy of
　currency, 50
　importance of trade to,
　　46, 49–50, 55–56
　golden age of, 55
　contributors to, 56–58
　drama, 62, 64
　education's contribution
　　to, 59
　end of, 66, 75
　philosophy, 59–60
　reasons for, 55–56
　rebuilding of Parthenon,
　　61, 63
　science, 64–65
government of
　Cimon's leadership of,
　　48–49, 50
　democratic, 30, 32–33,
　　40, 52, 75
　Pericles' leadership of,
　　50–54, 55, 60–61, 65
grooming habits in, 53
in Delian League, 47,
　48–50, 65, 67
in Peloponnesian War, 66
　aid to Corcyra, 67
　Long Walls, 52, 68,
　　69–70, 73, 75
　Spartan siege, 68–70
　Syracuse campaign, 66,
　　72–73
in Persian wars
　aid to Miletus, 35, 36
　battle of Marathon,
　　37–39, 40
　influence after, 44, 47
　Xerxes' invasion, 42
Macedonian capture of, 80
plague in, 70, 74
rivalry with Sparta, 44–45, 66
slaves in, 57
temperament of, 45, 47
wars with other Greek
　cities, 54
women in, 57–58

athletes, 27–28, 29
Atlantis, 16, 17
atoms, 65

Babylon, 82, 83
Barr, Stringfellow, 21
Bessus, 83–84
Bible, 90
Black Sea, 68, 75, 88
Bowra, C. M., 10, 15, 26, 30, 95, 98
Brasidas, 70
Breasted, James Henry, 46, 63, 86
Bronze Age, 12, 15, 21
Byzantium, 28

Capture of Miletus, The (Phrynichus), 35–36
Chaeronea, battle of, 80
Cimon
    military career of, 47, 48
    political career of, 48, 49, 50
city-states, 23, 24, 27, 28, 88
    after Peloponnesian War, 76
    conflicts between, 44–45, 49, 54
    evolution of democracy in, 30, 33
Classic Age, 11
Cleisthenes, 33, 52
Cleon, 70
Cleopatra, 94
Clouds (Aristophanes), 64
Colonne, Guido delle, 18
Corcyra, 67, 68, 69
Corinth, 28, 46
    relations with Sparta, 47, 54
    role in Peloponnesian War, 67, 68, 70, 72
Corinthian column, 56, 97
Cratarus, 87
Creasy, Sir Edwin, 38
Crete, 12, 15, 16
    see also Minoan civilization

Creticus, Heracleides, 89
Cyrus the Great, 34, 35

Dardanelles, 35
Darius I, 41
    attack on Athens, 36, 38, 39–40
    crushing of Miletus revolt, 35–36
    plan to conquer Europe, 34–35
Darius III, 81
    Alexander's defeat of, 82–83
    death of, 83, 84
debtors, 31, 32
Delian League, 47, 48–49, 54, 65, 67
Delphi, shrine at, 26–27, 80
democracy, 10, 24, 32
    in Athens, 44, 75
        evolution of, 30, 32–33, 40
        Pericles' contributions to, 52
    Spartan fear of, 45
    spread to other civilizations, 96, 97
Democritus, 65
Demosthenes, 79–80
Diadochi wars, 88
Dionysus, Theater of, 62
Dorians, 21, 22
Draco, 31, 32
Durant, Will, 26, 43, 53, 62, 93, 96

education, 59, 60, 78–79
Egypt, 33, 46, 50
    Alexander's influence in, 81–82
    Alexandria, 82, 88–90, 92–94
    civilization of, 10, 12, 29
    Ptolemaic kingdom in, 88, 89, 94
    rebellion against Persia, 54
    Rome's conquest of, 94

Ehrenberg, Victor, 31
Eratosthenes, 93
Eretria, 35, 36, 37
Euboea, 37, 54
Euclid, 93
Eumenes, 87
Euripides, 57, 62
Europe, 12, 34–35
    barbarians in, 88–89
    during Renaissance, 96
Evans, Sir Arthur, 14

foreigners, 31, 32–33, 78

Gauls, 88–89
geometry, 93, 97
Gerome, Jean, 10
gods and goddesses. *See* religion
government
    development of law, 31–33
    Greek contributions to, 10, 96
    in city-states, 30, 33
    service in, 52
    see also democracy
Greece
    agriculture in, 22, 28, 46
    Antigonid rule of, 88–89
    colonies of, 28, 30, 50, 68
    decline of, 89
    description of, 11, 22
    Gallic invasions of, 88–89
Greek civilization
    Alexander's spread of, 76, 82, 84, 86
    architecture of, 40, 42, 56, 60–61, 63, 87, 90, 91, 96–97
    art of, 27–30, 54–55, 87
    Athens's rise to power, 44–50, 54, 65
    city-states of
        conflicts between, 44–45, 49, 54, 76
        development of, 22–24, 28, 33
    dark age of, 21, 22, 28

grooming habits, 53
ideas of
    about individual worth,
        10, 24, 31, 52, 98
    in law, 30–33
    in philosophy, 59–60, 87,
        97
    Socrates' contributions
        to, 60
in Classic Age, 11–12
influence of, 11–12
    on ancient world, 87,
        89–94
    on European Renais-
        sance, 96
    on modern world, 96–98
    on Romans, 95–96
in Hellenistic Age, 87,
    89–94
language, 24–25, 87, 90, 97
literature of, 62, 64, 87
Minoan, 12–17
Mycenaean, 15, 17–19, 21
Peloponnesian War's im-
    pact on, 66, 68, 76
Pericles' influence in,
    50–52
Persian wars' impact on,
    34–43
playfulness of, 29
religion of, 25–27, 87
science of, 10, 64–65, 98
women in, 10, 32–33,
    57–58, 71
Greeks, The (Kitto), 23
Greek Way, The (Hamilton),
    29
Green, Peter, 78
gymnasium, 59

Hadrian, Emperor, 9
Hamilton, Edith, 29, 65
Hardy, W. G., 43, 49–50
Hector, 20
Helen of Troy, 18, 24
Hellenistic Age
    Alexandria's influence dur-
        ing, 89, 90
    architecture, 91

language, 90
science, 91–94
wars during, 87–88
Hellenization, 82, 84, 86
helots, 49
Herodas, 90
Herodotus's descriptions
    of Darius I, 34
    of Marathon battle, 39
    of Miletus's fall, 35–36
    of Thermopylae battle, 41,
        42
Heroes, Age of, 12, 25, 62
Hesiod, 23
Hipparchus of Nicaea, 91–92
Hipparete, 71
Hippocrates, 65
Homer, 19, 20, 23
hoplites, 37, 68, 80

Ictinus, 61, 63
Iliad (Homer), 19, 20, 25, 30
India, 83, 84, 85
Ionia
    freed from Persian rule,
        43, 47
    Persia's conquest of, 34–35,
        36
    see also Asia Minor
Italy, 28, 46, 72

Jews, 90
Jones, Archer, 37, 39

kings, 10, 30
Kitto, H. D. F., 23
Knossos, palace at, 12, 13–14

Labyrinth, 13–14
language, Greek
    development of, 24–25
    influence on modern lan-
        guages, 97
    use in Hellenistic Age, 87,
        90

law, 10, 24
    Draco's, 31, 32
    Roman, 96
    Solon's, 32
Leonidas, King, 9
    at battle of Thermopylae,
        41–42
Leucippus, 65
Leuctra, battle of, 76, 80
Levi, Peter, 40
literature and poetry, 31, 87
    basis of Greek, 19
    dramas, 62
    Pericles' support for, 54
    Roman, 96
Lives (Plutarch), 32, 51, 71
Luce, J. V., 16

Macedonia, 76, 77
    Antigonid rule of , 88–89
    conquest of southern
        Greece, 79–80
    fall to Romans, 94
    see also Alexander the
        Great; Philip II, King
        of Macedonia
Marathon, battle of, 37
    aftermath of, 40
    description of, 38, 39
Mardonius, 36, 43
Marinatos, Spyridon, 12
Megara, 54, 68
Menelaus, King of Sparta, 18
Miletus, 28, 35–36
military
    Archimedes' inventions
        for, 92
    Athenian, 45, 59, 66, 80
    hoplites, 37, 39, 41, 42, 68,
        80
    Macedonian, 76–78,
        81–85
    Persian, 34, 38, 39, 41
    phalanx, 77–78, 80, 83
    Roman, 94, 95
    Spartan, 30, 37, 41–42, 45,
        66, 70, 72, 75
    Theban, 80
Miltiades, 39, 47, 48

Minoan civilization
    art of, 12, 13, 14
    goddess- and bull-worship-
        ping in, 13, 14
    Mycenaeans and, 15, 17
    peaceful culture of, 13
    Theran eruption de-
        stroyed, 15–16, 17
Minos, King, 13–14
Minotaur, 13–14
Mitchell, Joseph B., 38
Mycenaean civilization
    compared to Minoan, 15
    conquest of Minoans, 17
    fall of, 21
    Trojan horse story, 18, 19

Nicias, 70, 72, 73
Nymphis, 88

Odysseus, 19
Odyssey (Homer), 19, 30
oligarchy, 30, 54
Olympias, 80–81
Olympic Games, 27–28, 29
ostracism, 40, 48, 50

palaces
    Minoan, 12, 13–14
    Mycenaean, 15, 17, 21
Palestine, 81, 88
Paris, Prince of Troy, 18
Parthenon, 40, 42, 54, 96
    rebuilding of, 61, 63
Patroclos, 20
Pausanias, 89
Payne, Robert, 13, 27, 52
Peace of Nicias, 70
Peach, Susan, 30, 58
Peisistratus, 30
Pellegrino, Charles, 17
Peloponnesian War
    effects of, 75, 76
    events leading to, 66–68
    Peace of Nicias, 70, 72
    siege of Athens, 69–70
    Sparta's winning of, 75

strategies at start of, 68
Syracuse campaign, 66,
    72–73
Perdiccas, 87
Pericles, 11
    building of Long Walls, 52
    death of, 70
    during Peloponnesian
        War, 67–70
    funeral oration of, 69
    golden age and, 55, 65
    Plutarch's description of,
        51, 58
    rebuilding of Parthenon,
        60–61, 63
    rise to power, 50
    views on women's roles, 58
Persian Empire, 33
    Alexander's conquest of,
        81–84
    alliance with Sparta, 75
    Delian League formed
        against, 47
    expansion of, 34
    Philip II's plan to invade, 80
    Seleucid rule in, 88
Persians, The (Aeschylus),
    42–43
Persian wars
    attack on Athens, 39–40, 42
    battle of Marathon, 37–39
    battle of Thermopylae,
        41–42
    conquest of Miletus, 35–36
persons
    Greek beliefs about worth
        of, 10, 24, 31, 52, 98
    Socrates' teachings about,
        60
phalanx, 77–78, 80, 83
Pharos (Alexandrian light-
    house), 90, 91
Phidias, 40, 61, 63
Phidippides, 37, 39
Philip II, King of Macedonia
    assassination of, 80–81
    conquest of Greece, 79–80
    unification of Macedonia,
        76–77
philosophy, 87, 97

Greek contributions to, 10
    teaching of, 59–60
Phoenicians, 25, 46, 50
Piraeus, 46, 48, 50, 52, 75
plague, in Athens, 70, 74
Plataea, 37, 70
Plato, 11, 16, 60
Plutarch, 14, 32
    on Alcibiades, 71, 72
    on Alexander, 76, 79,
        83–84
    on Cimon, 48
    on Demosthenes, 79
    on Pericles, 50, 51, 58
    on rebuilding of
        Parthenon, 61
poleis, 24, 27, 28, 88
    after Peloponnesian War,
        76
    evolution of democracy in,
        30, 33
Polybius, 89
Poseidon, 25
Ptolemaic kingdom, 88, 89
    fall to Rome, 94
Ptolemy, 87, 88

religion
    Greek
        characteristics of, 26
        festivals of, 27
        gods and goddesses of,
            25
        influence of, 87
        worship rituals in, 26
    Minoan, 13, 14
Renaissance, European, 96
Robinson, C. E., 57
Robinson, Charles Alexan-
    der, 10
Roman Empire, 9, 87, 92, 93
    Greek influence on, 95–96
    rise to power, 94
Rouse, W. H. D., 20

Salamis, Straits of, battle at,
    42–43
Schliemann, Heinrich, 19, 21

science
    during golden age, 64–65
    during Hellenistic Age,
        91–93
    Greek contributions to, 10,
        87, 98
Seleucid kingdom, 88, 89
    fall to Rome, 94
Seleucus, 87, 88
ships, 12, 42, 43
    Archimedes' inventions to
        move, 92
    Athenian, 44, 45, 49–50,
        52, 68, 69, 72, 73, 75
    importance of, 46
    in battles, 11, 42–43, 72–73
    Minoan, 12
    Persian, 36, 42–43
    Spartan, 75
slaves, 31, 49, 73
    Alexander's view of, 78
    contributions to golden
        age, 57
    exclusion from govern-
        ment, 32–33
Socrates, 11, 53, 58, 64
    teachings of, 59–60
Solon, 32
Sophocles, 11, 62, 98
    Antigone tragedy, 63
Sostratos, 90
Sparta, 28, 31
    government of, 30
    in Peloponnesian War
        alliance with Persia, 75
        relations with Corinth,
            67, 68
        siege of Athens, 68–70
        Syracuse campaign, 66,
            72–73
    in Persian wars, 37, 41–42
    influence after, 44
    loss of power, 49, 76
    market of, 23
    opposition to Delian
        League, 47, 67
    rivalry with Athens, 44–45,
        54, 65, 66–68

slave rebellion in, 49, 50
    temperament of, 45, 47
Sphinx, 82
Syracuse, 28, 46, 50
    Archimedes' inventions
        for, 92
    campaign at in Pelopon-
        nesian War, 66, 72–73

temples, 26–27, 61, 95, 96, 97
theater, 10, 62
Thebes, 28, 54, 68, 70, 72
    battle against Philip II, 80
    defeat of Sparta, 76
Themistocles, 52
    military career of, 42, 46
    political career of, 48
Theophrastus, 93
Thera
    towns on, 12, 18
    volcanic eruption at,
        15–16, 17
Thermopylae, battle of,
    41–42
Theseus, 14
Thessaly, 41, 79
tholos, 15
Thrace, 35, 36, 41, 75, 79
Thucydides, 44, 45
    on Delian League, 47, 49
    on Peloponnesian War, 66,
        69, 73
    on plague in Athens, 70, 74
towns. *See* city-states
trade
    among Minoans, 12, 15
    among Mycenaeans, 15,
        17–18
    embargo, 68
    importance of
        to Athens, 46, 49–50,
            55–56
        to Greeks, 22, 28, 30, 46
    in Hellenistic Age, 89, 90
Trojan History (Colonne), 18
Trojan horse, 18
Troy, 81

excavations of, 19, 21
    Greek seige of, 18
Troy and Its Remains (Schlie-
    mann), 21
Turkey, 18, 19
tyrants, 30, 40, 97
Tyre, 81, 94

*Unearthing Atlantis: An Archae-
    ological Odyssey* (Pelle-
    grino), 17
United States, 96, 97
    Greek influence in, 98

volcanoes, 15–16, 17

wars
    between city-states, 54, 65,
        67, 76
    Diadochi, 88
    Dorian, 21, 22
    justness of, 79
    Macedonian, 76–77, 79–85
    Mycenaean, 17, 20
    Peloponnesian, 66-75
    Persian, 35–42
    Trojan, 18–20
women, 18, 53, 71
    contributions to golden
        age, 57–58
    excluded from govern-
        ment, 32–33
    Minoan, 13
    priestesses at Delphi, 27

Xenophon, 58, 60, 75
Xerxes
    attack on Greece, 41, 42
    defeat at Salamis, 42–43

Zeus, 25, 27, 95

Picture Credits

Picture Research by Susan Hormuth, Washington, D.C.

Cover photo: North Wind Picture Archives

Culver Pictures, 69, 90

Historical Pictures/Stock Montage, 6, 36, 42, 44, 66, 75, 94

Library of Congress, 11, 18 (bottom), 19, 21, 24, 25 (both), 50, 56 (both), 62 (both), 64, 65, 83, 92, 97 (bottom), 98

The Metropolitan Museum of Art, Rogers Fund, 1914 (14.130.12), 27 (top)

Model constructed and photographed by Don Nardo, 61 (both)

National Archives, 97 (top)

Christine Nielsen-Nardo, 12, 15, 16, 18 (top), 22

North Wind Picture Archives, 9, 10, 14, 23, 27 (bottom), 28, 30, 31, 33, 35, 37, 39, 40, 41, 43, 45, 48 (both), 52, 54, 55, 57, 58, 59, 60, 67, 68, 70, 72, 73, 76, 77, 78, 79, 80, 81, 82, 84, 85, 86, 87, 88, 89, 91, 95, 96

About the Author

Don Nardo is an actor, film director, and composer as well as an award-winning writer. His writing credits include more than forty books, including *Gravity, Chernobyl, Anxiety and Phobias, The War of 1812, Eating Disorders,* and biographies of Charles Darwin, H. G. Wells, Thomas Jefferson, and William Lloyd Garrison. Among his other writings are short stories, articles, and teleplays and screenplays for ABC Television and feature films. Mr. Nardo, who is of Greek descent, is a lifelong student of Greek history and culture. He has traveled to Greece to examine many of the sites he writes about and has lectured extensively on the contributions of ancient Greece to the development of Western culture. He lives with his wife, Christine, on Cape Cod, Massachusetts.